EMMA GOLDMAN

# Emma Goldman

## *Revolution as a Way of Life*

VIVIAN GORNICK

Yale

UNIVERSITY
PRESS

New Haven and London

Published with assistance from the Louis Stern Memorial Fund.

Yale University Press books may be purchased in quantity for educational,
business, or promotional use. For information, please e-mail sales.press@yale.edu
(U.S. office) or sales@yaleup.co.uk (U.K. office).

Set in Janson Oldstyle type by Tseng Information Systems, Inc.
Printed in the United States of America by Sheridan Books,
Ann Arbor, Michigan.

The Library of Congress has cataloged the hardcover edition as follows:
Gornick, Vivian.
Emma Goldman : revolution as a way of life / Vivian Gornick.
p. cm.
Includes bibliographical references and index.
ISBN 978-0-300-13726-2 (alk. paper)
1. Goldman, Emma, 1869–1940. 2. Women anarchists—
United States—Biography. I. Title.
HX843.7.G65G67 2011
335′.83092—dc22
[B]
2011007549

ISBN 978-0-300-19823-2 (pbk.)

A catalogue record for this book is available from the British Library.

10  9  8  7  6  5  4  3  2  1

Frontispiece: Emma Goldman writing at her desk, ca. 1910. American
Pictorial Collection, Hoover Institution Archives, Stanford University.

# CONTENTS

# Part I

## *Temperament*

A HANDFUL OF RADICALS throughout the centuries have intuited that a successful revolution includes a healthy passion for the inner life. One of them was the anarchist Emma Goldman. The right to stay alive in one's senses, and to live in a world that prized that aliveness, was, for her, a key demand in any struggle she cared to wage against coercive government rule. The hatred she bore the centralized state was rooted in what she took to be government's brutish contempt for the feeling life of the individual. Fellow radicals who exhibited a similar contempt were to be held to the same standard. Comrades were those who, in the *name* of the revolution, were bent on honoring the complete human being.

Although Mikhail Bakunin, that fiercest of Russian anarchists, was one of her heroes, his famous definition of the revolutionary as a man who "has no interests of his own, no feelings, no habits, no longings, not even a name, only a single interest, a single thought, a single passion—the revolution" was as abhorrent to Goldman as corporate capitalism. If revolutionaries gave up sex and art while they were making the revolution, she said, they would become devoid of joy. Without joy, human beings cease being human. Should the men and women who subscribed to Bakunin's credo prevail, the world would be even more heartless after the revolution than it had been before.

The conviction that revolution and the life of the senses dare not be mutually exclusive made Goldman eloquent in defense of causes—sexual freedom, birth control, marriage reform—that a majority of her fellow anarchists derided as trivializing the Cause; the comrades repeatedly took her to task for, as many of them said, interpreting anarchism as a movement for individual self-expression rather than a revolution of the collective. Hotly, she defended her need to define anarchism as she experienced it, with or without radical consensus. After all, what good was a revolution if at the end of the day one couldn't speak one's mind freely? To retreat from *this* insight, she insisted, was to ensure political disaster. And, indeed, after the party of Lenin came to power in 1917—declaring the proletariat glorious, the intelligentsia contemptible, and any who said otherwise an enemy of the people—she knew that the Russian Revolution was lost. When she said so in Moscow in 1921, she was promptly invited to leave—exactly as she had been in the United States in 1919 after years of challenging the American democracy on much the same grounds. Keeping her company in one state of exile after another was the daily reminder—to herself and all who would listen—that the right to think and speak freely had always been the first article of faith nailed to Emma Goldman's front door.

It was the intensity with which she declared herself—in lecture halls, on open-air platforms, in school auditoriums and private homes, from theater stages and prison cells, the back of a truck or a courtroom stand—that made her world famous. That intensity, her signature trait, was midwife to a remarkable gift she had for making those who heard her feel intimately connected to the pain inherent in whatever social condition she was denouncing. As the women and men in her audience listened to her, a scenario of almost mythic proportions seemed to unfold before their eyes. The homeliness of their own small lives became invested with a sense of drama that acted as a catalyst for the wild, vagrant hope—especially vulnerable to mean-spirited times—that things need not be as they are.

This ability to make vivid the distress of living under the arbitrary rule of institutional power—Goldman's eternal subject, no matter what the title of the lecture—originated in an ingrained sense of oppression that burned as brightly in her at the end of her earthly existence as it did at the beginning. The story of her life, as she told it, set against a background of Russian despotism, Jewish marginality, and filial lovelessness, was one long tale of protest, not so much against poverty and discrimination (although there was plenty of that), as against a perception, there from earliest times, that some inborn right to begin and end with herself was forever being thwarted. There seemed always to be those in a position of authority to exercise restraint *unfairly, and for no real reason* over those who were not free to throw it off. She had always felt the situation as puzzling and unjust; and in her, such was her disposition, that injustice burned unbearably. It was the "unbearably" that set her apart.

In short: Emma Goldman was a born refusenik. "Don't tell *me* what to do!" must have been the first sentence out of her mouth. An anecdote made famous in the 1970s when Goldman's iconic status was being revived says much on this score. One night when she was young, she was dancing madly at an anarchist party when a puritanical comrade urged her to stop, insisting that her frivolity was hurting the Cause. On the instant,

Emma flew into a rage, stamped her feet, and told him to mind his own damned business. "If I can't dance," her response has been paraphrased, "I'm not coming to your revolution." The tale is told as a tribute to the emblematic boldness with which she defended her right—everyone's right—to pleasure, but it could just as easily have concentrated on the startling extremity with which she balked at restraint and swiftly felt hot defiance boiling up inside her.

*Felt* is the operative word. She always claimed that the ideas of anarchism were of secondary use if grasped only with one's reasoning intelligence; it was necessary to "feel them in every fiber like a flame, a consuming fever, an elemental passion." This, in essence, was the core of Goldman's radicalism: an impassioned faith, lodged in the nervous system, that feelings were everything. Radical politics for her was, in fact, the history of one's own hurt, thwarted, humiliated feelings at the hands of institutionalized authority. Handed down from on high, such authority was to be fought at all times, in all places, with all one's might. From this single-minded simplicity—one that neither gained nuance nor lost force—she never departed. It was, in her, a piece of inspired arrest.

There are at least two ways to make vivid the claim that Emma Goldman might have on the attention of the contemporary reader. One is to write a political history of her years as they unfolded both in Europe and America, showing in detail how her contribution to world anarchism speaks to our own time; the other is to concentrate on the force of her extraordinary rebelliousness and try to understand it in light of the existential drive behind radical politics. This biography is engaged with the second of these approaches.

Anarchism itself is a protean experience, as much a posture, an attitude, a frame of mind and spirit as it is a doctrine. Conventionally defined as a political theory that opposes all forms of government and government restraint, anarchism advocates voluntary cooperation and the free association of individuals and groups in order that all social needs be met. Within that basic construction of political thought there exists a distinct division between the anarchism of collective living and that of the individual. The first is concerned with class struggle and the success of the commune, endorsing an economic system organized around cooperative, worker-owned enterprises and a social system devoted to strict egalitarianism; the second is passionate about the inner liberation of the individual. Both kinds of anarchists believe that under anarchism, as each conceives it, every negative in the human disposition (greed, envy, irrational malevolence) will disappear, and with that disappearance will go every social humiliation: injustice, inequality, exploitation. If people *feel* free and equal, the anarchist insists, order and cooperation will emerge as a natural result of that beneficence. Above all else, the anarchist is out to prove that cooperation, not competition, is the natural impulse of the human race.

Emma Goldman was a hybrid anarchist. Although she was formed by European (communistic) anarchism, and spent her life denouncing the state, she had a passion first for the work of the German philosophers of individualism (Friedrich Nietzsche and Max Stirner) and then for that of American dissenters like Henry David Thoreau and Walt Whitman whose romantic defense of the supremacy of the individual spoke even more directly to her emotional imagination; it was out of the language of the homegrown American rebel that her anarchism found its great expressiveness and defiant originality. This passion for individuation, as old as the Greek discovery of consciousness, burned in her not only as an angry hunger to feel free within her own self but as an undying insistence that that freedom was a human birthright. To live in a world that denied one's birthright was the intolerable prospect that fed her rebelliousness and, in turn, led her to the kind of insight that contributed substantially to the never-ending inquiry into the question of what a human being needs to feel human.

She was born in 1869, in the imperial Russian city of Kovno, into a family of low-grade Tolstoyan unhappiness. Neither rich nor religious, the Goldmans were shopkeeper Jews endowed with temperament. Marked by outsiderness of every kind, their lives were nonetheless driven by a hunger for an emotional satisfaction that, like everything else they sought, remained just beyond reach. Emma's mother, Taube, had been married at fifteen to a man she had loved; when he died, leaving her with two young daughters who meant less to her than the beloved dead husband, she brooded on her loss. A second marriage was quickly arranged, this one to the volatile Abraham Goldman, who also had a fantasy of love. When he saw that Taube was not going to supply it, he went into a permanent rage. She responded with scorn, and then withdrew into a remoteness that neither Abraham nor the children could penetrate. The marriage evolved into a vicious stand-off whose tensions permeated the life of the house.

It did not help matters that Abraham was also unworldly, squandering the money that Taube had brought into the marriage (her daughters' inheritance) in one losing venture after another; he bought a grocery, managed an inn, invested in a dry-goods store, but whatever he touched fell to pieces. As Emma reported in her autobiography, the family moved constantly, from Kovno to Konigsberg to Petersburg, but wherever they went, Abraham failed. Into the bargain, he had persuaded himself that if their firstborn was a male, his inclination to failure would be mitigated. Ultimately, three sons came of this benighted union, but the first child was Emma. It was Abraham's habit throughout their young lives to beat his children when they displeased him. With Emma he used a whip.

The whip was necessary because in this child Abraham had encountered a capacity for wounded outrage that matched his own. Possessed of a spirit that apparently could not be molded—she *would* discover things for herself—Emma was experienced as uncontrollable. Nothing could force from her the one thing Abraham desperately needed: obedience. "I'll kill her," he would howl when the young Emma set her will against his; "I'll kill that brat!" Determined to subdue her, as she grew from infancy to adolescence he resorted to ever increasing despotism, either hitting her with his fists or making her stand in a corner for hours on end, throwing her against the wall or having her walk repeatedly across a room holding a glass of water for which she would be beaten if one drop were spilled. The more despotic Abraham became, the more resistant Emma grew. She never begged, she never cried. Instead, she took her punishment in a way that drew his admiration and his fear. Like him, she lashed out.

Emma was indeed the wild child. Mad for school—for this she *had* begged—nonetheless, here, too, her need to challenge homegrown tyranny *on the spot* was stronger than her need to succeed as a student. Enrolled in a primary school in Konigsberg, she did battle with the teachers she thought abusive—one beat the children's hands with a ruler, another tried to molest the girls, a third humiliated them verbally—and, inevitably, punishment without appeal was the outcome. Although she passed the exam to secondary school, she was denied the character reference necessary for admission—the religion teacher declared her "a terrible child who would grow into a worse woman"—and that gave her father the excuse he was looking for. When she was twelve, Emma's formal education came to an end. At thirteen she was working in a glove factory, at fifteen in a corset factory. It was here that she began to learn what it meant to be of the class that has no rights, only obligations.

These experiences proved formative; and the fact that they

*were* formative is illuminating. Like all young girls, Emma day-dreamed sexual attention, romantic love, foreign adventure; but unlike other young girls, these daydreams were not where she lived. By the time she was fourteen she had begun to conceive of life as a power struggle of a vast and primitive order. This vision captured her imagination as did nothing else, aroused in her the strongest of feelings. It was exciting to feel strongly. More than exciting: compelling. She knew instinctively that to follow the depth of emotion that social injustice induced in her was to engage with her most responsive self; she also knew that it was through that responsiveness that she would get where she determined to go. Deep within, in a place not yet made conscious, Emma knew that it was not domestic happiness she craved, it was the world: to be in it and of it, to there make her mark.

People like Emma Goldman, with their timeless hunger for living life on a grand scale, are born every hour, on the hour, but only rarely does the hunger last beyond earliest youth, much less find itself fed by a personality of enduring passion driven to intersect aggressively with its moment. For those so endowed, there remains only the time it takes to discover the idiom in which the great adventure is to be lived out.

Political radicalism was Emma's first romance not only because it suited her temperament; revolt was in the very air she breathed, growing up as she did in the imperial Russia of the 1870s and 1880s—many of her adolescent contemporaries also daydreamed themselves on the barricades. Writers and teach-ers, students and artisans, aristocrats and civil servants—for forty years they'd all been debating the possibility of joining the modern world by overthrowing the monarchy in the disci-plined pursuit of one utopian vision of socialist reform or an-other. In 1863 a radical intellectual named Nikolai Chernyshev-sky published an explosive novel, *What Is to Be Done?*, that laid out a program of social change that promised sexual liberation, an economy based on social justice, and egalitarianism on every level. To achieve this peaceable utopia, Chernyshevsky's novel posited, its protagonists must become single-minded, Bakunin-style activists. The hero has no wife, no friends, no conversation; he eats raw meat, sleeps on nails, and lives as though hunted. The influence this novel exerted on two generations of Russian radicals (one legendary reader was Lenin) is often compared to that of *Uncle Tom's Cabin* on the growth of abolitionist sympathies in the United States in the years leading up to the Civil War.

When the teen-aged Emma read *What Is to Be Done?* twenty years after it was first published, she instantly identified with Vera, the female protagonist who runs away from a middle-class home, joins a radical cell, and lives and dies for the revolution. Emma herself, however, was not destined to join the revolt brewing in Russia. For her an extended education in radical rage—one that would replace one romance with another—was waiting to conclude itself with the Ur-experience of America, day by immigrant day. It was amid the tenements and factories of Rochester, New York, in 1885 that the radicalizing of Emma Goldman would complete its apprenticeship.

Her father had announced that it was time for her to marry—she was nearly sixteen—and he would arrange things. Objecting (violently, of course), she begged, once more, to be allowed to go back to school. Whereupon Abraham spat at her, "All a Jewish girl need know is how to make gefilte fish, cut noodles fine, and give her husband babies." She begged to be allowed to immigrate to America with her sister Helena (the only relative whom she loved), where the two of them could join their older sister, Lena, already living with a husband and children in upstate New York. No! said Abraham, and Emma, in the incomparable Yiddish phrase *Zi vaftzikh fun die vendt,* proceeded to "throw herself from the walls." When she finally threatened suicide, he shrugged—all he really wanted was to get her out of the house—and said okay, go.

From the moment the two girls landed at Ellis Island, where they were treated like enemy aliens—"Guards roughly pushed us hither and thither, shouted orders to get ready . . . the atmosphere charged with antagonism and harshness, nowhere could one see a sympathetic official face"—it was obvious that they were not leaving the old life behind. Without money, education, or language, Emma and Helena soon discovered, they were condemned to the same indentured servitude they'd known in Europe. No, not the same: worse. Here, the exercise of money power had achieved a starkness that made them look back on the disorganized meanness of Saint Petersburg factories with something like nostalgia. Industrialization in this country, completed within fifty years of the Civil War, had been undertaken with an unparalleled speed and brutishness, generating an immense amount of human fallout. Together, the speed and the fallout were American capitalism in all its rapacious particularity. On the one hand, you had the famously openhearted New World welcome to all who knew how to capitalize on high risk venture; on the other, you had the vicious treatment of all whose labor must be exploited in order to bring the venture to fruition. It was here, in the belly of the beast, that the word *sweatshop* came to represent hell on earth.

Throughout most of the nineteenth century and well into the twentieth, millions of immigrants lived as though they were members of a subhuman species, in unspeakable filth and poverty in the tenement districts of large American cities, working twelve hours a day, often seven days a week, sewing clothes in sweatshops equivalent to, if not worse than, the tenement hovels in which they ate, slept, and procreated.

The essence of the sweatshop, however, was not even the in-humanity of the hours and the working conditions; it was the practice of "sweating" the workers. At the end of an eighty-hour week in a dark, crowded, filthy shop, a worker who was sewing sleeves into blouses at five cents a dozen might think she had earned four or five dollars, but then she would find that she was being charged for the thread and needles she used, the sewing-machine power she generated with her feet, the chair on which she sat, and the locker in which she stored her coat and handbag. Even when the large loft factories came in at the turn of the century, the crowding was still terrible, the hours were just as primitive, and a worker was fined if she went to the toilet, fined if she was five minutes late to work, fired if she complained about the bad light, the crowded floor, the filthy bathrooms. The small humiliations that ate into the soul re-mained in place.

Not only had America turned out to be the same hell the Goldman girls had crossed an ocean to escape; in these and other ways it proved more devastating. Here, workers and bosses alike were uneducated immigrants. This meant that only yesterday many of the factory owners themselves had been the people sitting at the machines. Yet now they were treating the people at the machines as though they were less human than themselves. And then again, there was the shock of so many of these factory owners being Jewish. The Goldmans had lived all their lives in a world of ghetto Jews that, despite a certain amount of wealth distribution, had been able to count, in some rough measure, on tribal allegiance; but here in America class trumped ethnic solidarity to a degree never before imagined. Not only had the experience of powerlessness, as immigrants and as Jews, not implanted a shred of fellow feeling in factory owners; it demonstrated that to gain power was, inescapably, to become a predator oneself. As Hannah Arendt would some eighty years later observe grimly, "The humanity of the insulted and injured has never yet survived the hour of liberation by so much as a minute."

The system was slavery, pure and simple; that much was clear. The crime of such slavery, Emma now began to see even more clearly, was that it induced a level of humiliation that, as Marx had rightly said, was spiritually deforming. People survived by shutting down inside, a development that led to alienation not only from the world but, infinitely worse, from oneself. It was an experience from which nobody emerged intact.

Around the same time that Emma was thinking out these equations of class, slavery, and humiliation in Rochester, halfway around the world, in Moscow, Anton Chekhov, brooding on his own miserable experience as the grandson of a serf and the son of a religious fanatic, was pondering much the same dilemma and concluding that while others had made him a slave, he alone could squeeze the slave out of himself—and, at that, only drop by drop. If Emma had been able to subscribe to *that* analysis, she might have become an artist; as she could not, she became a revolutionary. It was not, her pent-up feelings told her, up to the enslaved to free themselves psychologically; it was up to them to force change on the system. What now followed were three years in which she battled her way into enough clarity on this insight to make of it the basis for a way of life.

Within a year of Emma and Helena's arrival in Rochester—as though to mimic their already exploded hopes of the new world—Abraham and Taube followed the girls to the States, thereby reestablishing their wretched family life. Now the two young women worked nonstop. Emma sewed overcoats for more than ten hours a day, earning two and a half dollars a week, in one miserable factory after another to support the aged parents in a treadmill existence that soon made it impossible for either of the girls to imagine a future different from the joyless present.

At one of her jobs she met Joseph Kershner, a fellow worker who shared her love of books and her hatred of the work. After a few months of walking and talking together, Kershner convinced her that they should marry. She was eighteen years old. Except for her sister, who was not intellectually inclined, she hadn't a soul in the world to talk to. Why not, she thought. On their wedding night she discovered that her husband was impotent, and suddenly she saw the marriage for the act of desperation it had been. It was not just that Joseph could not get an erection; he was a terminally depressed man who had been drawn to Emma in the forlorn hope that her vitality would rescue him from himself. True to form, Emma then flew to the farthest extreme, associating marriage itself with failed sexual love. "If ever I love a man again," she swore silently, "I will give myself to him without being bound by the rabbi or the law; and when that love dies I will leave without permission."

Emma left her husband within months of the wedding and sued for divorce. This piece of boldness so unbalanced the chaotic Goldmans that she was induced to return to Kershner, which she did, even going so far as to marry him a second time, only to leave him again a few months later (without benefit of a second divorce), this time for good. Living once more at home, and now at painfully loose ends, she took refuge in the sense of coherence with which her interest in radical politics had always supplied her. She began to read more systematically than she had in Europe and to attend the meetings of the various kinds of radicals storming about in Rochester. The socialists were persuasive, but their presentation of the problem was, for her, uninspired. The anarchists, on the other hand, were instantly exciting. It was the vividness with which they made you *feel* social injustice that captured her emotional attention. One night she came home from an anarchist meeting so aroused that she wakened Helena, who listened with amusement to the rush of words pouring out of her. "The next thing I'll hear about my little sister," Helena said, "is that she, too, is a dangerous anarchist." Only a catalyst was needed to set Goldman's life on its path; and as though on cue, along came the Haymarket affair, an event very nearly calculated to embody the primitivism of class warfare.

In the last decades of the nineteenth century and the first of the twentieth, all over Europe as well as in America, as the heartlessness of Victorian industrialism deepened in coal mines and clothing factories, steel mills and lumber camps, wherever roads and houses and bridges were being built, a desperation of relations between those who owned and those who labored was growing ever more deadly. Whenever worker protest mounted, hired guns—often aided by the local police, national guards, or state troopers—appeared to shoot at, jail, blacklist, and, if necessary, kill the protesters and their organizers; and everywhere, the workers replied in kind: with guns of their own, or even dynamite, the poor man's only real source of return fire. Thousands of people on both sides of the divide perished during these years, and thousands more instantly took their place. The labor movement grew slowly—spilling blood, rage, and resistance in equal parts—but it grew. Between 1881 and 1906 more than thirty thousand strikes and lockouts took place in America alone, involving over nine and a half million workers, and affecting thousands of businesses of every sort. Hundreds of these confrontations ended with state or federal troops being called in. Every time a major strike took place—almost always accompanied by a massacre of one kind or another—the larger meaning of this war between the classes politicized untold numbers: again on both sides of the divide.

In 1884, the fledgling Federation of Organized Trades and Labor Unions (with headquarters in Chicago) had resolved that eight hours should constitute a legal day's work, and that if national legislation did not endorse this resolution by May 1, 1886, a general strike would be called. The deadline came and went without Congress's having acted on labor's ultimatum, and what came to be known in American labor history as the Great Upheaval took place. Almost half a million workers, led by radicalized unions, participated simultaneously in more than fourteen hundred strikes nationwide.

On May 4, 1886, a rally was held in Chicago's Haymarket Square in support of the striking workers. At the end of a peaceful evening of protest—mainly on behalf of some workers who had been killed the day before—a pipe bomb was thrown into a line of police. The cops opened fire on the crowd, and within minutes the dead, including seven policemen and eleven demonstrators, littered the streets. Eight of the Chicago labor leaders, all self-described anarchists, were charged with the crime and, although it was almost a certainty that none of them had thrown the bomb, a trial was begun that lasted a year and a half, gained the attention of the world, and ended in November 1887 with the hangings of four men whose deaths would become iconic in American labor history. On the scaffold one of them, August Spies, cried out prophetically, "The day will come when our silence will be more powerful than the voices you strangle today!"

Eighteen-year-old Emma Goldman was beside herself. She had followed the story religiously in the pages of *Die Freiheit*, a German-language publication from New York edited by the militant anarchist Johann Most. Nothing held her attention as closely as Most's inflammatory prose: "lava shooting forth flames of ridicule, scorn, and defiance." Years later she said that it was Most's analysis of the Haymarket trials that had crystallized her political understanding.

On the day of the hangings she felt "thrust into a stupor; a feeling of numbness; too strong for tears." Later that evening at her father's house a relative sneered, "What's all this lament about? The men were murderers. It is well they were hanged," and Emma leaped at her throat. Someone cried, "The child has gone crazy!" Whereupon Emma threw a pitcher of water at the woman's face, screaming, "Out, out! Or I will kill you!" and dropped, weeping, to the floor.

The strength of her own emotion shook her, but that night she realized she had become an anarchist. An incandescent light had gone on in her head. She saw, as in a vision, that the hangings called for nothing less than resistance of a high and dramatic order. Along with Louis Lingg, one of the hanged labor leaders, she knew the despair and the excitement of wanting—no, *needing*—to "reply with dynamite."

Emma Goldman never got over that flash of insight. It was her moment of conversion, or, as she later called it, her epiphany. Radical fire had at last been ignited in her, and the light and heat that it generated made her understand herself in a way that she had not before. It was an awakening that came like revelation.

Many, if not most, children exhibit an early talent for art or science, even intellection; but we can never accurately predict the one in whom the youthful giftedness will develop into a driving need of the kind that determines the course of a life. In creative work, the driving need occurs when the talent is exercised: the possessor of it finds that she or he is struck to the heart (not a thing that happens simply because one has talent), and a sense of expressive existence flares into bright life. That experience is incomparable: to feel not simply alive, but expressive. It induces a conviction of inner clarity that quickly becomes the very thing one can no longer do without. (If it can be done without, it usually is.) Those destined for a life of professional radicalism experience themselves in exactly the same way as does the artist who reaches center through the practice of the gift. No reward of life, not love or fame or wealth, can compete. It is to this clarity of inner being that the radical, like the artist, becomes attached, even addicted.

This, I think, is what happened to Emma Goldman the night that the Haymarket labor leaders were hanged. Theirs was the cause that told her, not approximately but precisely, who she was. Within the year anarchism would become emblematic of that which gave definition: the reflection of the expressive self that she could no longer do without.

On a Sunday morning in August 1889, twenty-year-old Emma Goldman arrived in New York City with a sewing machine under her arm and five dollars in her pocket. She had three addresses in her bag: the first, that of a distant aunt and uncle; the second, of an anarchist student whom she'd met once; the third, Johann Most's *Freiheit* offices. She went initially to the aunt and uncle, whose uneducated timidity made them greet her with a diffidence she found insulting. Unable, as always, to tolerate even a moment's frustration—"the bitterness that filled my soul over the cruel reception given me by my own kin"—she left within the hour, fleeing to the student, who welcomed her enthusiastically, and took her right down to Sachs's Café on the Lower East Side, where, as *Die Freiheit* had already informed her, every anarchist in the city hung out. Within the hour she had met Alexander Berkman, who would become the most important person in her life, and fallen in with a group of his friends, who invited her to share their apartment, and she was taken that same evening to listen to Johann Most, the man who would initiate her apprenticeship as a public speaker. She was grateful to the student, but it is probably the last time in her life that she would need an intermediary.

The speed with which Emma felt herself folded into the communal life of the young would-be revolutionaries milling around lower Manhattan in the 1890s—all immigrants, all speaking Russian or German or Yiddish—was actually unremarkable, given the time and the place. Across the world their counterparts were gathering in ever-growing numbers in much the same way. Emma and her friends could have been living in Petersburg or Paris, London or Berlin, Zurich or Budapest, for all that the city in which they actually worked imprinted on them. A sense of shared political urgency, alive to the touch in Europe and Russia as well as in America, made it reasonable for these people to think of the coming revolution as a universal certainty, and that certainty became the home they never left. Wherever they landed, they ate, drank, and slept revolution. The jobs they held—driving trucks, sewing clothes, baking bread—were in every sense of the word day jobs. Revolution was who they were and what they did.

In the United States at this time a colorful and varied native radicalism that had been brewing for decades dovetailed with many of the sentiments of international revolutionaries. It included the stirring presence of the democratic reformer Jane Addams, who worked for change through electoral politics; the Industrial Workers of the World (IWW) leader Big Bill Haywood, who vowed to make a clean sweep of the entire capitalist system; the utopian socialist Eugene Debs, who ran for president and to many seemed an American holy fool. Together they created and sustained an atmosphere of political agitation, either liberating or disorienting, depending on what you stood to lose or gain, that seemed to promise permanent upheaval. Among those who were ignited by the turbulence were many who despaired of peaceful social change and saw no way around committing what the anarchists called "propaganda by the deed"; these were the suicide bombers of their day, and there were enough of them floating around the world that between 1880 and 1910 six heads of state (including one U.S. president) were assassinated.

Nonetheless, homegrown socialism grew rapidly in

America after the turn of the century. On the eve of the First World War there were more than three hundred socialist publications—dailies, weeklies, monthlies, in English and in foreign languages—originating in every part of the country. More to the point, between 1902 and 1912 the Socialist Party's membership swelled to well over a hundred thousand, and socialists were able to deliver nearly a million votes to Eugene Debs when he ran for president in 1912.

Even though they thought of themselves as citizens of the world, Emma and her friends—nearly all of them Jewish—felt most at home on New York's predominantly Yiddish-speaking Lower East Side, where the sociology of world radicalism was replicated in miniature. A small, densely populated part of the city, the area was famous not only for its "teeming masses" (those fabled immigrants supposedly waiting only to become true-blue Americans) but for this army of radicals (socialists, anarchists, unionists) whose presence in the neighborhood was as familiar a sight as that of the grocer, the rabbi, the night-school teacher. "Uptown" remained foreign territory, an abstraction where capitalism incarnate resided, but here in lower Manhattan immigrant radicals swam like fish in the sea, vividly present when aboveground and easily camouflaged when not, but either way exerting an influence disproportionate to their numbers.

Between 1881 and 1914, two million Jewish immigrants arrived in America; the majority of them headed straight for New York's Lower East Side. The tenements, the streets, the life itself were choked with noise, dirt, and poverty, as well as something never experienced in Europe: expectations. Here, during these years, a whole Yiddish-speaking world had been brought to life, complete with newspapers, synagogues, and cafés; sweatshops, theaters, and whorehouses; peddlers, gangsters, social workers. In this tight little world it was radicalism that seemed to offer the first light at the end of the long tunnel that émigré Jews had entered upon leaving Europe for the Promised Land.

Central to this culture was a hunger for learning that increased exponentially as generation after generation of the newly arrived poured onto the streets of the Lower East Side. By the thousand they went to night school, to the Yiddish theater, and above all, to lectures. "God, those lectures of ours!" remembered one immigrant fifty years after he arrived in the States. He heard poets and professors, Zionists and philosophers, Yiddish nationalists and American reformers, each clamoring for his attention and his allegiance. Ignorant but intelligent, he felt that he needed to learn from each and every one of them: "So when Zhitlovsky talked about Herbert Spencer — you can imagine how badly we needed Herbert Spencer on Delancey Street in those days! — I listened." He could hardly make sense of any of it, but "I thought to myself, maybe next time I can swallow it all," even though for the longest time "I didn't know where one thing began and the other ended. What was the connection between Herbert Spencer and the Vilna Gaon?"

The people who had no trouble explaining the connection between Spencer and the Vilna Gaon (as well as the one between filthy capitalism and their miserable lives) were, of course, the radicals. The only way you'll put it all together, they assured this immigrant, is to join us.

There wasn't an hour of the day or a day of the week in the 1880s and 1890s when one could not hear a socialist speech of one variant or another, not only in a lecture hall or at a mass meeting but on street corners and in squares and parks all over the East Side.

From anarchism to social democracy, the left-wing project was woven into the expanded expectations that America aroused in its vast, unlettered immigrant life. For those who were temperamentally disposed, socialism was, in fact, the school without walls that they attended. In its unflagging attempt to make proletarians out of workers, socialism offered an explanation of one's life that embraced the entire human enterprise. Daily, as one Jewish immigrant remembered it, on every street corner on the Lower East Side, *Kultur*, spewing from the soapboxes, "erupted like an active volcano" delivering in a radical context "religion and atheism, free love and vegetarianism, politics and ideologies."

To a remarkable extent, the political animation alone provided the critical mass necessary for each socialist persuasion to first articulate itself and then figure out where it stood in relation to life in the new world. The left-wing response to America—both the idea of the Golden Land and the reality— ran an extraordinary gamut, but in the end it was social democracy, with its unambiguous desire not to destroy but to participate in the existing political system, that commanded the devotion of the majority of those who felt a need to take political action. The head of the Buffalo branch of the Socialist Labor Party spoke for many when he told a reporter in 1887, "When I was in Russia I was a nihilist and advocated violence and did my share in the movement. But in this country . . . I regard it as madness and criminality to counsel violence in a place where men can speak and write and vote. . . . Here the ballot is every man's weapon."

Yet in these years, among Jewish radicals none were more dynamic than the anarchists, who in their unaccommodating view of capitalist reality often struck the note most emotionally satisfying. These were women and men who considered the reasoning of social democrats delusional. For them neither electoral politics nor union building, to which the democrats were devoted, could *ever* achieve any significant transformation of capitalism, much less bring about socialist revolution. To the anarchist, whose head seemed permanently filled with blood, "armed struggle and armed struggle alone" could liberate the workers from the slavery of the system. These were people convinced beyond argument that there was no negotiating with capitalism. One must strike hard and fast, and with the single-minded intention of destroying the state so thoroughly that it could never rise again.

The Jewish anarchists were the intensely secular children of a religion-based culture they experienced as unforgivably passive in the face of world injustice. Although industrial capitalism was the main enemy, organized religion ran it a close second, and wherever and whenever one could, one made a defiant gesture in that direction. Throughout the 1880s and 1890s, Lower East Side socialists of every persuasion held masquerade balls to celebrate, commemorate, and raise money. The most outrageously provocative were the anarchist balls, invariably held on Yom Kippur, the holiest day of the Jewish year. In time, none would dance more wildly at these affairs than our protagonist.

And it is here that we rejoin the young Emma Goldman on her first day in New York City in the summer of 1889.

Drinking coffee with Alexander Berkman and his friends in Sachs's Café (a room full of wall-to-wall political argument), Emma was home free: at last among her true kin, living on streets she thought of as hers, in the midst of a dailiness of political activism that would, in and of itself, be family to her for the rest of her life.

Sasha (as Berkman was known throughout his life) was a year younger than Emma and, like her, a Jew from Kovno. Unlike Emma, Sasha was well read, intellectually inclined, sensually fearful, and extraordinarily doctrinaire. He leaned across the coffee cups, looked directly into her eyes, and, his didactic voice cutting through the noise of the café, began his instruction in the need for radical severity. "Nothing personal mattered," Emma wrote of the Sasha she met that first day in New

York. "Only the Cause mattered. Fighting injustice and exploitation mattered." Emma's eyes shone as she listened to him, the uncompromised orthodoxy thrilling her down to her little black boots.

In some ways, the rigid, bespectacled, sexually innocent, theoretically advanced Berkman remained as he was at nineteen. In him, too, the emotional arrest was inspired. Years later, in his *Prison Memoirs*, he supplied what was still his favorite self-description: "Could anything be nobler than to die for a grand, a sublime Cause? Why, the very life of a true revolutionist has no other purpose, no significance whatever, save to sacrifice it on the altar of the beloved People. And what could be higher in life than to be a true revolutionist? It is to be a *man*, a complete MAN. A being who has neither personal interests nor desires above the necessities of the Cause; one who has emancipated himself from being merely human, and has risen above that, even to the height of conviction which excludes all doubt, all regret; in short, one who in the very inmost of his soul feels himself revolutionist first, human afterwards."

Ultimately, Berkman's life was shocked into a more comprehensive view of human existence. At the age of thirty-six he emerged from a fourteen-year incarceration in a turn-of-the-century American prison as ardent an ideologue as ever but also a man in whom emotional understanding had penetrated flesh and bone and reached the heart. Sasha lived to become a much-loved figure among the anarchists, unusual for the breadth of his interests and the depth of his sympathies.

Not surprisingly, when Sasha and Emma met he was a disciple of Johann Most's, and worked for him at the *Freiheit*. That very evening the two entered a neighborhood saloon whose back room was filled with German-speaking radicals, there to hear the fiery anarchist speak; Justus Schwab, a German anarchist famous among radicals for his nobility of character, was the keeper of this saloon, and in time Emma would become a regular at this place (for years, it was her mailing address) where the avuncular German was fond of observing affectionately that her head was made not for a hat but for the rope.

She was prepared to idolize Most before she ever laid eyes on him. In the Rochester press he had been called "a devil, a criminal, a bloodthirsty demon!" That was good enough for her. Johann Most was then in his early forties, and at first sight physically repellent. A man of medium height, he was possessed of an overly large head surrounded by bushy gray hair that framed a face whose left side was hideously deformed. Women almost always shrank from him. Not our Emma. For her the blue eyes were magnetic, the voice was richly compelling, and oh! the rhetoric. Most spoke that night of American conditions in general—"No country was ever more suited for anarchist agitation than present-day America"—and of the Haymarket massacre, which should have made guerrilla activists out of every left-winger in the world: "What socialist, without flushing with shame, now maintains he is not a revolutionary?" he thundered. "We say: none!" Emma was immensely excited by a speech riddled through with "scorching denunciation, biting satire, passionate tirade," and a speaker who himself was "transformed into some primitive power, radiating hatred and love, strength and inspiration."

Johann Most was born in Germany in 1846 and, like Goldman herself, had very young begun to boil. He never for a moment believed in reform through parliamentary action; for him, it was in-your-face rebellion all the way. Eventually, he served brief prison terms in half the countries of Europe before landing in the United States. In London, in 1881, he did a year and a half of jail time for publishing a "red" *Freiheit*—the paper was literally printed in red—in which he registered his boundless delight over the assassination of Tsar Alexander II.

No sooner had Most arrived in New York than he set up the offices of the *Freiheit* and was soon distinguishing himself as the first anarchist in the States to speak openly and favorably of *attentat*, political assassination. "The existing system will be quickest and most radically overthrown by the annihilation of its exponents," he stated categorically. "Therefore, massacres of the enemies of the people must be set in motion." In time, he predicted, it would be necessary for anarchists preparing for social revolution to "use every means—speech, writing, or deed, whichever is more to the point—to accelerate revolutionary development." Most was an essence of the insurrectionary anarchist. In America he was jailed at least three times.

Emma was enchanted. "He stirred me to my depths," she wrote years later. The next day Sasha took her up to the *Freiheit* offices, where Most, in his turn, was charmed by the fresh-faced young woman whose own blue eyes were filled with open adoration. "Come back next Wednesday," he said. Alone, was what he meant. When she did, they went out for coffee, and he immediately took the opportunity to do what he never would have done if she had been a man: poured out his (sexually scheming) heart. "Yes, little girl," he sighed. "Idolized by many, but loved by none. One can be very lonely among thousands. Did you know that?" Emma was touched and moved—stirred, in fact, to her very depths—for which read, manipulated and seduced; in all probability she slept with him, as she no doubt did with other of the comrades who came on to her in the same way.

In no time at all, Emma and Most, speaking German together, were hanging out, seeing each other almost daily. Now, *she* was pouring out her heart, and he, of course, had to listen to her. He might have been bored—he probably was to begin with—then something unexpected happened. As Emma's voice filled the air between them with dramatized tales of her own wretched childhood, Most found himself startled, and impressed, by her storytelling abilities. Everything she described came not only to vivid but to meaningful life. As she was incapable of reciting the particulars of an event or a circumstance without making some larger sense of them, nothing was simply the sum of its own limited parts. He began to see her as a disciple who could deliver the anarchist message for him, and one day he burst out, "I will make you a great speaker—to take my place when I am gone." Emma was startled by the suggestion but soon easily won over to Most's perception of her as one worthy of speaking for the Cause and of the immense value of speaking: "The spoken word, if hurled forth with eloquence, enthusiasm, and fire, could never be erased from the human soul." The spoken word at this time was almost always in German; for Emma, it would not be in English until the mid-1890s.

Within a month of Most's impetuous outburst, she was instructed to take his place on the lecture circuit and sent out on tour, first to Rochester, then Buffalo and Cleveland. Thus, she arrived back in the city she had left just six months before, in her own eyes a person who had "lived years in that time," but in reality an anxious fledgling. When Helena met her at the train station and realized the path that Emma was now embarked on, she could not contain her dismay. Whereupon Emma flared, "My life is my own!" Actually, her life was not yet her own—but soon, very soon . . .

The lecture was billed as a talk on the keenest issue of the working-class moment: the eight-hour day. For Johann Most, this was a bogus issue. He had things on his mind: the overthrow of the *entire* capitalist system. He wanted Emma to urge the workers who would come to her talk to see the futility of this minor struggle and to bend all their efforts toward the larger revolution. He had, in fact, written her speech for her.

Emma got up to speak in Rochester, and her mind went blank. Most had equipped her with phrases that were foreign to her—"the iron law of wages," "supply and demand," "poverty as the only leaven of revolt"—and, looking into a roomful of silent, hard-worked faces, she suddenly found, mumbling and stumbling, that she could not speak them. It wasn't that she disagreed with what the words were saying; it was just that they weren't *her* words; and because they weren't hers, they sounded thin and abstract in her own ears, refusing to make connective sense in that place in her mind where, when allowed spontaneity, the words multiplied rapidly and naturally. In a panic, she decided to scrap the prepared speech and talk straight "from the heart." In a moment she felt her own reality and was soon associating freely to the past, easily invoking the horrors of working-class life as she had ever known them: "In a flash I saw it—every incident of my three years in Rochester: the factory, its drudgery and humiliation, the failure of my marriage, the Chicago crime. The last words of August Spies. I began to speak. Words I had never heard myself utter came pouring forth, faster and faster. They came with passionate intensity, they painted images. . . . The audience had vanished, the hall itself had disappeared; I was conscious only of my own words, of my ecstatic song."

The tired workingmen were electrified. Their applause broke over her head. She was stunned. Of a sudden she saw that she "could sway people with words!" and she exulted (more than exulted: she "wept with the joy of knowing"). But when the clapping had faded away that first night in Rochester, from out of the audience came a lone voice: "Inspiring speech, but what about the eight-hour day?" Just as quickly as she had soared, Emma now subsided in confusion, and was instantly cast down. "I've failed!" she cried to herself. Eloquence was not enough. She had not given these people what they wanted, what they needed.

She went on to Buffalo, determined to give the audience what it had come for, but once again, at the conclusion of her speech she saw that she had failed. Unable to address the subject as Most had laid it out for her she again spoke from the heart, yet could not find within herself a form of speech that satisfied. Although she had done better here than in Rochester, her mentor's words had repeatedly paralyzed her efforts to speak naturally. In Cleveland she resorted to sarcasm, scorning the workers' stupidity in concentrating on such trifles as the eight-hour day. When she said this there was a momentary silence, and then a worker in the audience, thin-faced, white-haired, said he understood her impatience with such small demands as the eight-hour day—after all, she was young, what were a couple of hours more or less to her?—but he could not wait for the overthrow of the entire capitalist system; right now he needed two hours less of work a day to feel human, to read a book or take a walk in daylight. That did it. Something snapped, and the hold of Johann Most's words on her mind was broken.

The experience was life changing. It was the moment when Emma Goldman began to create "Emma Goldman." She knew instinctively, from the moment the thin-faced worker had said he needed two hours more a day to himself, that she must make come to urgent life the immediate and the concrete, and that she must do it by transforming her own experience so compellingly that those listening would taste in their mouths the condition under which they themselves labored. To do this— and again her instinct was infallible—she must find (or make or fashion) a dramatic persona, drawn from her own ordinary, everyday self, who could tell the story she now felt she had been born to tell. She had to teach herself not only how to develop this persona but how to equip it with a voice that could move persuasively from pedestrian reality to world reality to anarchist reality and then back again. And of course she did. Years later, it was easy enough to see, as one generation of radicals followed another, that she had done it better than any number of firebrand speakers put together.

In *The God That Failed* the novelist Richard Wright gives a memorable description of a 1934 Communist Party meeting in Chicago (actually, it's a trial for expulsion) at which a number of organizers speak. The first gives "a description of the world situation . . . [painting] a horrible but masterful picture of Fascism's aggression in Germany, Italy, and Japan"; the second invokes the "Soviet Union as the world's lone workers' state, hemmed in by enemies"; then the third speaks of "the domestic situation in the United States [linked] with the world scene" and the fourth "of Chicago's South side, its Negro population, their sufferings and handicaps, linking all that, also, to the world struggle." At last, pictures of the world, the nation, and the neighborhood "had been fused into one overwhelming drama of moral struggle in which everybody in the hall was participating . . . [and] had enthroned a new sense of reality in the hearts of those present, a sense of man on earth. With the exception of the church and its myths and legends," Wright concludes, "there was no agency in the world so capable of making men feel the earth and the people upon it as the Communist party."

Within three years of that first lecture tour, Emma Goldman had made herself into a speaker who, in her own finite person, could do all of the above so well that J. Edgar Hoover soon considered her "the most dangerous woman in America."

When Emma returned to New York in the winter of 1890, she went to dinner with Most. By now, he was in love with her, and his interest in her as a political comrade was on the back burner. He showed up at the restaurant on that cold February evening dressed in a natty suit, his beard trimmed, with a bunch of violets in his hand. Her absence, he told her, had been unbearably long, he never should have let her go just when they'd grown so close. Emma was startled. This was not the kind of attention she'd been looking forward to. Here is her own account of that fateful dinner:

"I tried several times to tell him about my trip, hurt to the quick that he had not asked about it. He'd been so eager to make a great speaker of me; was he not interested to know whether I had proved an apt pupil?" Yes, of course, he replied, but he'd already received reports on her eloquence and her quick-wittedness. "'What about my own reactions?' I asked. 'Don't you want me to tell you about that?' 'Yes, another time.' Now he wanted only to feel me near . . . his little girl-woman.

"I flared up, declaring I would not be treated as a mere female. I blurted out that I would never again follow blindly, that I had made a fool of myself, that the five-minute speech of the old worker had convinced me more than all his persuasive phrases. I talked on, my listener keeping very silent. When I had finished, he called the waiter and paid the bill. I followed him out. . . . On the street he burst into a storm of abuse. He had reared a viper, a snake, a heartless coquette, who had played with him like a cat with a mouse. He had sent me out to plead his cause and I had betrayed him. I was like the rest, but he would not stand for it. He would rather cut me out of his heart right now than have me as a lukewarm friend."

Emma begged him to understand, but by now Most was out of control. "Who is not with me is against me!" he shouted. "I will not have it otherwise." Then Emma herself began to scream. And she could scream. Most became frightened, and fled. Horrified by the whole episode, Emma returned to the communal apartment, collapsed in tears, and related the story of the evening from beginning to end. For a moment, the comrades were silent. She imagined the silence to be a form of sympathy for the abuse she had just suffered. Then Sasha blurted out, "Violets at the height of winter. With thousands out of work and hungry!"

Emma stared at him. A pox on all of you, she thought. Yes, violets in winter, and other people's words be damned. I'll speak my own piece, or no piece at all.

Her apprenticeship as an amateur refusenik was at an end. From that night forward she would be a professional.

The remarkable extremity of thought and feeling exhibited among all the principals—Emma, Most, Sasha—that winter night in 1890 was, among anarchists, not an aberration but rather a prerequisite, one that owed its character to the larger-than-life original, Mikhail Bakunin, whose explosive ardor had become symbolic of the movement as a whole.

Modern anarchism—that is, anarchism that names itself as such—began when Bakunin's followers split the 1872 Hague meeting of the International Workingmen's Association (IWA) in noisy opposition to the control of the organization by Karl Marx. The split had been a long time coming, and when it did, the consequence was dramatic: two conflicting strands of socialist thought and action (the Marxist and the anarchist) emerged—and the untimely demise of the First International was accomplished.

The IWA had been founded at a meeting in London in September 1864 for the express purpose of deciding on active struggle to gain economic justice and political rights for workers the world over. One of those present was Marx, who at that meeting—where it was decided that rules, a constitution, and a General Council would be drafted—did not speak at all. But a month later, Marx managed to manipulate himself into a position wherein it fell to him to write the address to the working classes for the first major congress, and he took the opportunity to rewrite the by now agreed-upon rules to suit himself. Like many another self-styled prophet, Marx was a master politician in the mean as well as the capacious sense of the word.

That first congress, held in Geneva in 1866, was attended by members of various left-wing groups operating throughout Europe in the wake of the 1848 revolutions—Italian republicans, German social democrats, French Proudhonistes, English

Owenites. The sound of strong-minded disagreement filled the hall. Though in time the IWA became a remarkably successful organization with some eight million members and branches all over the continent, it was characterized from the start by conflict. It was only in 1868, however, when Bakunin and his friends joined the organization, that the conflict escalated from quarrels into war. Marx, now solidly entrenched in the influential General Council, was a dominating force in the IWA, and at this time he was committed to the goal of producing a disciplined, class-conscious proletariat that would form a party of its own and become a power in parliamentary politics. For Bakunin, such a prospect was death. Either it was all-out revolution, or the organization might as well close its doors right now, he said. And kept on saying.

Mikhail Bakunin was born into Russian nobility in 1814 and reared to become either a soldier or a civil servant. Yet—once again!—we have in him a creature marked from earliest life by a restlessness and a rebelliousness that went so deep they made him cut loose at twenty-one, when he left home in single-minded search of a way to live a meaningful life: that is, a life that would enable him to ferret out a systematic way to understand the world not as it was but as it should be. There followed a frenzy of ideological obsessions, the first settling on religion, the second on pan-Slavism, the third and last on revolutionary socialism, with the emphasis on revolutionary. From the beginning, Bakunin's was a socialism characterized by an overwhelming desire to have humankind make an entirely fresh start. To clear the way for such an occurrence, it was necessary to dismantle the world as he knew it. By the age of thirty-two he was already proclaiming, "The passion for destruction is a creative passion." Which suited the times marvelously.

From the 1840s on, Bakunin was involved in so many revolutionary uprisings throughout Europe that within a decade he was wanted in three countries. Wherever rebellion flared, he was sure to arrive within minutes, join the action, and urge the protesters to stay the course, no matter how bloody the end might be. A story is told that when the uprising began in Dresden in 1848, Bakunin, who had been about to leave town, instantly did an about-face and joined the rebels. As the king's men closed in—on what would prove to be one of the worst defeats of the year for European revolutionaries—Bakunin (as he later told the young Richard Wagner, who'd also been in Dresden at the time) urged the provisional government to "blow itself up, together with the town hall, for which I had enough gunpowder." But, he shrugged, they didn't want to. Instead, they fled, and Bakunin left town.

When he was finally caught in 1849 he spent a year in detention, first in Austria, then in Germany, and was then handed over to the Russians, who imprisoned him in the dreaded Peter and Paul Fortress, the prison that stands on a patch of land in the middle of the Neva River, facing Saint Petersburg. This prison was Russia's Devil's Island. Here, Bakunin languished for some five years (at one point chained to a wall for two months) until the tsar responded to pleas from his wellborn family and he was exiled to Siberia, where he managed a legendary escape in 1861, slowly making his way, via Japan and the United States, back to Europe.

By the mid-sixties, his thoughts having clarified throughout the years of enforced removal from the political scene, Bakunin had become devoted to an idea of socialism that would be guided *solely* by the urge to secure the absolute freedom of every individual on earth. Nothing mattered except the right to total self-determination: at all times, in all places, under all circumstances. The "absolute rejection of every authority [that] sacrifices freedom for the convenience of the state" was key. *Absolute* was his favorite word.

Bakunin, as the historian Paul Avrich puts it, was "the prophet of primitive rebellion." He longed for a true "revolt of the masses," the more unforgiving the better. The social revolution, he declared, would "not put up its sword before it had destroyed every state across our whole civilized world." Himself gargantuan in body as well as in spirit and rhetoric, he wanted to mount a giant uprising that would include the lumpen and the peasantry as well as the factory workers, and act like a tidal wave, drowning the world of the state in floods of rage. He most hoped, Avrich notes, to live long enough to see "the spontaneous rising of infuriated urban mobs driven by an instinctive passion for justice and by an unquenchable thirst for revenge."

An unquenchable thirst for revenge.

What was most electrifying about anarchists like Bakunin was the depth and the breadth of their emotional anger, rising up as it did from the psychological deeps, as though with the force of an inner awakening to something evil about life itself that was reflected in the inequities of organized society. Many (like Bakunin himself) experienced the exercise of *any* authority as a form of intolerable oppression; indeed, anarchism's ultimate contribution to modern political thought may be the gloriously excessive identification of authority, in and of itself, as an instrument of oppression. Just listen to the sound of this magnificent rant by the great French anarchist Pierre-Joseph Proudhon:

> To be governed is to be kept in sight, inspected, spied upon, directed, law-driven, numbered, enrolled, indoctrinated, preached at, controlled, estimated, valued, censured, commanded, by creatures who have neither the right nor the wisdom nor the virtue to do so. To be governed is to be, at every operation, every transaction, registered, taxed, stamped, measured, assessed, licensed, authorized, admonished, forbidden, reformed, corrected, punished. It is, under pretext of public utility, and in the name of the general interest, to be ransacked, exploited, monopolized, extorted, squeezed,

mystified, robbed; then at the slightest resistance, the first word of complaint, to be repressed, fined, despised, harassed, tracked, abused, clubbed, disarmed, choked, imprisoned, judged, condemned, deported, sacrificed, sold, betrayed; and to crown all, mocked, ridiculed, outraged, dishonored. That is government; that is its justice; that is its morality.

This is language both mad and exhilarating, brave and absurd, heart sinking and heart swelling, language that seems to speak directly to a sense of insult and injury—perhaps inborn in the race itself—that periodically gathers overwhelming strength in the face of those social inequities that both reflect and extend the existential grievance. When a moment in cultural time arrives that a critical mass of people is consciously identified with that grievance, the language in which it first expresses itself is, inevitably, that of Bakunin and Proudhon.

In 1970, at a time when social unhappiness seemed to be erupting all over the United States, a young radical said, "The New Left today comes upon Anarchy like Schliemann uncovering Troy." Reading those words in the twenty-first century, one realizes that this was a sentiment that resonated strongly with the sixties counterculture as a whole, and the liberationist movements in particular. Suddenly, in those politically aroused years, everyone in America who felt "sacrificed, sold, betrayed"—from Bakunin ever-readies like Abbie Hoffman down to the most traditionally obedient of women or gays—everyone was adopting the speech and tactics of antisocial rebellion. Thinking back, for instance, as this biographer surely can, to the raging intemperateness of exploding radical feminism—"Marriage is an institution of oppression!" "Love is rape!" "Sleeping with the enemy!"—one can easily see that the first feminists of the 1970s and 1980s were primitive anarchists. They didn't want reform, they didn't even want reparations; what they wanted was to bring down the system, destroy the social arrangement, no matter the consequence, under which women had lived for centuries as second-class citizens. When asked (as they were, repeatedly), "What about the children? What about the family?" they snarled (or roared), "Fuck the children! Fuck the family! We're here to declare our grievance, and make others feel it as we do. What comes later is not our concern." In the main, these were women of the law-abiding middle class who, at this crucial moment of unmediated revolt, were sounding like professional insurrectionists.

*Unmediated* was the operative word in the 1960s and 1970s—and not for activists alone. The prevailing spirit of unmanaged release acted not only as a prod to break up social ossification but as a catalytic reminder of something deep in the human psyche that, ironically, attracted even as it alienated, and was as beckoning to the ordinarily respectable in the late twentieth century as it had been in the late nineteenth. When anarchism as a political presence was at the height of its power and influence in the United States—between 1890 and 1920—the tumult it caused, with the unending accusations it leveled against capitalism and the state, electrified thousands of ordinary citizens who were excited and repelled in almost equal parts by the open voicing of the kind of antisocial feeling that in benign times conjures up Huckleberry Finn lighting out for the territory but in threatening times Joseph Conrad's secret agent, and at all times calls your attention, whoever you are, to those impulses that you spend your life actively stifling. Now, when you were confronted (swamped, invaded, deluged) by social rebels—in your face morning, noon, and night—the sheer concentration of outrage in them took your breath away. There was in it something primeval: some undiluted purity in the nay-saying that thrilled even as it dismayed.

Therein lies the tale, I believe, of America's decades-long obsession with Emma Goldman, as reflected in the love-hate affair with her that the American press carried on for more than thirty years. For tabloid journalism, Emma, seen at once as free spirit and bomb thrower, was that irreducible essence, resistance itself. The reporters couldn't get enough of her. She aroused in them fear and admiration, scorn and curiosity, longing and contempt. They reviled and insulted her—and tipped their hats to her by printing nearly every word she spoke.

In August 1893, at the height of one of America's worst depressions—tens of thousands unemployed, rally after rally demanding government relief, a hunger march on Washington—Emma had given one of her most provocative speeches. Standing on an overturned packing box in New York City's Union Square, she cried out (probably in German) at a crowd of five thousand, "Men and women, do you not realize that the State is the worst enemy you have? It is a machine that crushes you in order to sustain the ruling class, your masters. . . . It is the pillar of capitalism, and it is ridiculous to expect any redress from it. Do you not see the stupidity of asking relief from Albany with immense wealth within a stone's throw of here? Fifth Avenue is laid in gold, every mansion a citadel of money and power. Yet there you stand a giant, starved and fettered, shorn of his strength. . . . Wake up. Become daring enough to demand your rights. Demonstrate before the palaces of the rich. Demand work. If they do not give you work, demand bread. If they deny you both, take bread. It is your sacred right."

Emma was at her best badgering and berating her working-class audience. They loved being told that all they had to do was fight their own cowardice. Her insulting bluntness was received like balm applied to an open wound. Eyes glittered with relief as she scorned those listening for not taking to the streets *now*, right now. Inevitably, the applause was deafening, and a sea of hands reached up toward her, as though to touch her was to gain spiritual strength.

"Red Emma!" the afternoon papers screamed that summer

day in 1893—"Her vitriolic tongue is just what the ignorant mob needs to tear down New York!"—and they printed every word of the speech.

The following week she was arrested on a charge of inciting to riot and sentenced to one year in the penitentiary on Blackwell's Island, now Roosevelt Island, in the middle of New York's East River. Like many another revolutionary, Emma put the time in prison to good use, learning English and acquiring some nursing skill, thus emerging from incarceration stronger than ever in spirit, if not body. When her time was up she stood outside the prison gates, the newspaper reporters gathered around her. What now, Emma? they called out tauntingly. You finished raising hell, Emma? She raised her head defiantly—she was still only twenty-five years old—her cheeks red, her eyes ablaze. "Society is in its last convulsions," she announced, as if just finishing the Union Square speech of the year before. "Men cannot be happy as long as they are slaves. They cannot expect theft, murder, prostitution, or oppression to be gotten rid of unless the system which breeds them is gone. . . . For this I shall continue to work. My motto as ever [is] 'Death to Tyranny! Vive l'Anarchie!'"

She had just served a prison sentence for giving, almost verbatim, this same speech in Union Square. The doors of the prison behind her could easily have opened and she be yanked right back in. But no power on earth could have stopped her from speaking her mind. Her need to do so was insurmountable and unquenchable. It was this—the insurmountable and the unquenchable—that kept the press hungry for anything to do with her. The words she spoke that day were part of a prison letter she had written that the New York *World* subsequently published in full, its editors announcing that they had bought it as they would have bought an unpublished poem by Tennyson or a description of a prize fight by John L. Sullivan—that's how emblematic a creature she seemed to them.

From the moment in 1890 that she had opened her mouth in Rochester to address a roomful of working-class men until the moment she disappeared into the mists of deportation in 1919, Emma-Goldman-in-America was front-page news. True, overexcited coverage of radical politics in a time of enduring class warfare would inevitably have made Emma a staple of tabloid journalism; but as garish and brutish as the newspaper writing of those years was, it still betrayed a strange and rather moving complexity of motivation with regard to her words, her person, her extraordinary suggestiveness.

For the press, Emma was never just a political speaker, she was always a "rabid female agitator." She did not simply talk, she delivered "wild, bloodthirsty harangues." Emma was regularly referred to as the Queen of Anarchism—she who "Rules with a Nod the Savage Reds"; it was as though anarchism was an outlaw territory and Emma its guerrilla leader. One newspaperman loved to call her "the Petroleuse," after the women of the Paris Commune who used petroleum to set fire to buildings when the Commune was under siege.

In 1901, after a deranged anarchist assassinated President William McKinley, Emma was arrested in Chicago and held for two weeks on suspicion of complicity, of which she was not guilty. Headlines blared across the country. One of the longest, fullest accounts of her arrest appeared on the front page of the Chicago *Tribune*, illustrating perfectly the wild mixture of anxiety and admiration she routinely aroused in those reporting on her.

Here, in bold, is how the story was headlined on the front page:

EMMA GOLDMAN IN LAW'S GRASP
High Priestess of Anarchy Found Hiding in Chicago
FACES OFFICERS CALMLY
Admits She Met the Would-be Assassin Here on July 12

but Denies She Has Seen Him Since
Reiterates That Violence Is Not Her Creed and Declares
"McKinley Is Too
Insignificant A Man" to Kill.

The *Tribune* piece then went on to describe her arrest in the dramatic terms reserved for the capture of known criminals, also providing (at extraordinary length) an account of her background, along with her views on love, marriage, the inequality of women, the meaning of political violence in the face of ongoing social injustice, and her taunting behavior in the police station. "If they want to keep this up," she said to the reporters concerning the interrogating police, "why, let them go ahead. They are making Anarchists by the dozen. They will save me much work."

And then, just when Emma was sounding most provocative and the reporter most belligerent, the tone of the story suddenly underwent a change, and the reporter began describing, with admiration, Emma's appearance as she was being led into the police chief's office. "Her short walking skirt of blue cloth had been carefully brushed, her white waist was spotlessly clean, the band of blue silk ribbon knotted about her neck was held in place by a jeweled pin. Her hair, light and parted, was brushed back, and gave her the appearance of a student—an appearance further heightened by the heavy, gold bowed eyeglasses which she wore. . . . Paleness marked her cheeks at times, but there was never any evidence of fear. Her slight Polish accent and the rolling of her 'r's' betray her birthplace—Russia. It lends, however, a fascination to her speech."

The absorptive interest in Emma's person is telling. It was as though in narrating the story of her appearance the writer was hoping to puzzle out something that he could neither understand nor dismiss. Over a period of more than twenty years, nearly every piece on her of any substantial length described in great detail her manner, her dress, her bearing. Sometimes these descriptions were used to humanize, sometimes to demonize, but always to help the reporter clarify on a take that seemed to elude him.

A feature interview in the New York *World* in July 1892 describes the reporter finding Emma sitting in a corner at the back of Justus Schwab's saloon, her feet up on a chair, reading peacefully in a roomful of hard-faced, hard-drinking men. She is pronounced pretty, with chestnut-brown hair "fluffed over her forehead, leaving only a trace of the part," possessed of "a trim figure, five feet four or five inches tall, well moulded with hard flesh [hard flesh!], clothed in a white blouse, tan-colored belt and a gown of blue sateen striped with white, and tan shoes." Then the reporter gets to work: "She has a shapely head; a long low white forehead; light bluish-gray eyes, shielded by glasses; a small, finely chiseled nose, rather too wide at the nostrils for symmetry; a colorless complexion; cheeks that once had been full, but now are slightly sunken, giving a moderately pinched appearance to a face that loses its beauty [with] the rapid decline to the chin. The mouth in repose is hard and sensual, the curves gross, the lips full and bloodless. . . . A neck that once was rounded was still well poised, but as she turned her head the tendons bulged out into scrawniness, and blotches here and there added to the sharp disappointment one meets with after leaving the upper part of her face." When she smiled the interior of her mouth looked black or, rather, "that dull opaque hue characteristic of the mouths of some snakes." Ah! Now he's nailed it.

As the men in the bar grow restive (the interview is going on too long), one of them pronounces, in a German the reporter understands, that all reporters should be killed: "She smiled that hollow cavernous smile, her eyes shone behind her glasses. A glad and proud look was on her face, and while she made a faint display of quieting her slaves her pale face took on some color and she stood there wreathed in smiles amid smoke and beer fumes."

But some journalists (and here's the love part of the love-hate affair), mocking their colleagues' queen-in-hell approach to Emma, found her enchanting—Nellie Bly, for instance, one of the New York *World*'s most prestigious reporters. Interviewing Goldman in prison in the early 1890s, Bly told her readers that she, like they, had never met the famous anarchist before but, she asked sardonically, did they really need an introduction to Emma Goldman? After all, "You have seen supposed pictures of her. You have read of her as a property-destroying, capitalist-killing, riot-promoting agitator. You see her in your mind a great raw-boned creature, with short hair and bloomers, a red flag in one hand, a burning torch in the other, both feet constantly off the ground and 'murder!' continually on her lips." When Goldman was actually standing before her, Bly "gasped with surprise and then laughed" at a young woman she instantly found appealing. For two hours Bly let Goldman talk about capitalism and anarchism, personal freedom and sexual love, buying books instead of clothes—"Think of that, you girls who put every dollar upon your backs!"—until at last she pronounced Goldman a "modern Joan of Arc."

Across the country, throughout the volatile 1890s, in small-as well as big-town newspapers, the most unexpected of appreciations would crop up. Toward the end of the decade, a reporter at the nonpartisan San Francisco *Call*, as smitten with Emma as was Nellie Bly, urged his readers to go hear her speak, even if it meant missing an evening in which Nellie Melba was singing or Sarah Bernhardt acting, as she (Emma) was the most interesting woman they were ever going to hear. "Had she lived a century ago," the writer enthused, "she'd have been beheaded, two centuries ago . . . given over to the loving embrace of the *jungfrau* (the 'iron maiden'), while in the sixteenth century nicely boiled in oil or broken on the wheel. . . . She has life, she has courage, she has brains. She is fiercely consistent, unwaveringly true and, though I can't agree with her, I believe her to be absolutely sincere."

There are, of course, obvious differences between the anarchism of Emma Goldman's time and that of the 1970s. In her time, anarchism was a serious element in a worldwide movement for political revolution—an ideology that spoke to tens of thousands of people across the classes and around the globe—and those who gave their lives to the dream of an anarchist future often endured expulsion, prison, death. In the 1970s, anarchism was a posture, an attitude, a way of protesting the transgressions of a democracy that most rebels wanted to see made more perfect; it was a revolution in consciousness rather than in the system that they were after. Nonetheless, the anarchists of both periods—rejecting militarism, corporatism, nonegalitarianism—were devoted to the ideal of personal liberation, and advocated direct action as opposed to gradual change. All were committed to pushing hard at the boundaries of political protest until they reached the limit beyond which protest would be tolerated—and then pushing even harder. For those who went beyond the limit, life offered a tumultuous sense of the heroic that often exploded in one's face when, suddenly, the receptivity of the time having passed and the crowds having gone home, you found yourself out there alone. This, too, was an experience shared by the anarchists of 1970 with those of 1920: many in both periods never came in from the cold.

It is the irony of the professional revolutionary's life, sworn to the cause of a peaceful new social order, that it should be lived continually in a state of tumult that passes for liberation, in the midst of a mob scene that passes for comradeship, until the action dies away, whereupon the revolutionary finds him- or herself at a severe inner loss. When the all-embracing turmoil of the sixties subsided and the national passion for resistance for the sake of resistance had exhausted itself, thousands were lost: there was not a place in the world where they felt at ease inside their own skins. Emma Goldman, living out her revolutionary life on a far more dramatic scale, was equally sealed into an existence that was posited on the receptivity of turbulent times; and she too suffered immensely when that receptivity died away. Inevitably, the revolution that didn't get made condemned the anarchists who had defied every authority, cut every tie, rejected citizenship itself to wander the earth feeling, as Goldman put it, "nowhere at home."

Indeed. These were personalities made for citizenship in the country of Nowhere at Home.

When he was entombed in the Peter and Paul fortress, Bakunin was asked to make a confession (that is, to name names). He refused in a rambling letter to the tsar that included a startling reflection on his own psychological makeup. "In my nature," he wrote, "there has always been a basic flaw. . . . Most men seek tranquility; in me, however, it produces only despair. My spirit is in constant turmoil, demanding action, movement, and life. I should have been born somewhere in the American forests, among the settlers of the West, where civilization has hardly begun to blossom and where life is an endless struggle against untamed people, against untamed nature—and not in an organized civic society."

In short, what Bakunin needed was permanent revolution: revolution as a way of life. And so did Emma Goldman.

# Part II

## In the Life

THINK WEATHERMEN—the breakaway group of the new left for whom, in the late sixties, "propaganda by the deed" had become a compelling reality—and you've more or less got the mood of Sasha and Emma and their friends, still in their early twenties, in the first years of the last decade of the nineteenth century. Self-styled revolutionaries for whom industrial capitalism had daily become more viscerally intolerable (especially for Sasha), they were living inside an emotional pent-up-ness— easy to describe, almost impossible to analyze—that would soon require relief. So strong was this feeling of righteous rage that it projected itself onto what they imagined was a waiting world. Wherever they were, however they were putting body and soul together—sewing clothes, working in an ice cream parlor, learning to typeset—they were essentially occupying a crash pad, waiting for the moment (almost here!) that would signal the start of the general uprising.

And then came Homestead.

In June 1892, a Carnegie steel plant in Homestead, Pennsylvania, became the focus of national attention. The current agreement between owner Andrew Carnegie and the Amalgamated Association of Iron and Steel Workers was about to expire, and the union presented management with a new wage schedule. Carnegie was away in Europe, but the plant manager, Henry Clay Frick, had full powers of arbitration. Destined to become one of the richest men in America, Frick was a fierce opponent of organized labor; he refused to recognize collective bargaining and announced that he would, in fact, no longer deal with the union at all. The workers immediately went out on strike—and Carnegie Steel went to war. Frick closed the plant, laid off all the workers, evicted their families from company housing, and told them that they would have to apply individually for their jobs if they ever wanted to come back to the plant. The striking workers, insisting on their right to organize and to deal collectively, won universal sympathy, even from the conservative press, which declared their tone "manly." Frick remained unmoved. Strikebreakers were brought in, and along with them guards from the Pinkerton agency. On July 6 a fight broke out between three hundred Pinkertons and a crowd of armed unionists. During a twelve-hour gunfight, seven guards and nine strikers were killed. The country as a whole condemned the Pinkertons and supported the strikers.

Emma and Sasha were tremendously excited by these developments—"To us," she wrote years later, "it sounded like the awakening of the American worker"—and when Sasha pronounced this "the psychological moment for an attentat," she glowed. Together, they decided, they would go to Homestead and assassinate Frick.

While Sasha was trying—and failing—to fashion a homemade bomb, Emma, absurdly enough, tried to raise money for clothes, a weapon, and a ticket to Pittsburgh, none of which they had, by selling herself. "If sensitive Sonya [in Dostoyevsky's *Crime and Punishment*] could sell her body," she reasoned, "why not I?" But she was so awkward at it that her first night out on the street a kindly man took her into a saloon, bought her a beer, gave her ten dollars, and told her to forget it, she didn't have the knack. Eventually, it was her sister Helena who, upon being told that Emma was sick, sent the necessary money.

In the end, it was decided that Sasha alone would carry out the deed, and Emma would remain behind to explain their action to the world. Like children concocting a heroic scenario, neither one could have had a grasp on the sober reality of what they were about to do. So off Sasha went with a gun and a knife concealed within the jacket of the strategically purchased new suit, and, remarkably, on July 23 he gained entry to Frick's office where he shot Frick three times, then stabbed him in the leg, and still failed to kill him! Sasha himself was instantly beaten to the ground and held there until the police arrived; he was amazed that the very workers he had expected to join him in what was clearly a call to "direct action" had helped to subdue him. Apparently the awakening of the American proletariat was not quite as near at hand as Sasha and Emma had expected.

Henry Frick survived. If he hadn't, Sasha Berkman would have been executed. As it was he was sentenced to twenty-two years in prison—many more than the number usually meted out for attempted murder—and his life took its dramatically altered course. Jail made Sasha wise in more ways than one. He came, first, to a vivid understanding of prison life as a replica in miniature of all that was pathological in the organized world, and then to a realization of all that was incalculable in human psychology. "The attitude of the guards toward the [inmates]," he wrote in a journal that became a memoir, "is summed up in coercion and suppression. They look upon the men as will-less objects of iron-handed discipline, exact unquestioning obedience and absolute submissiveness. . . . [A]uthority and remuneration . . . is awarded to the guard most feared by the inmates and most subservient to the Warden—a direct incitement to brutality, on the one hand, to sycophancy, on the other." At the same time he was deeply moved to see how dramatically mixed was the basic humanity of the so-called common criminal, witnessing as he did acts of depravity and acts of decency committed repeatedly by the same inmate. And then, at the last, he saw what was really hard to swallow: that despite the desperation inherent in all this institutional hell, no American, however low on the social scale, would ever grasp the good of attentat. "In Russia," he wrote, "where political oppression is popularly felt, such a deed would be of great value. But the scheme of political subjection is more subtle in America." In Europe the "autocrat is visible and tangible," but here in the New World, the "despotism of republican institutions is far deeper, more insidious, because it rests on the popular delusion of self-government and independence. That is the subtle source of democratic tyranny and, as such, it cannot be reached with a bullet."

If Berkman himself could not readily submit to this hard-earned piece of wisdom—for the rest of his life he would walk a tightrope of calculated opinion on the question of attentat—Emma Goldman certainly could not. She never again, after Homestead, endorsed political assassination, but neither would she condemn it. Declaring repeatedly that anarchism as a philosophy was opposed to violence, she nonetheless blazed when political assassination was denounced by those she considered ignorant or ill-informed. In a lecture that she gave quite often, "The Psychology of Violence," she avowed openly, "The man who flings his whole life into the attempt, at the cost of his own life, to protest against the wrongs of his fellow men, is a saint compared to the active and passive upholders of cruelty and injustice, even if his protest destroys other lives besides his own." What was not properly understood, she felt, was that the forces of authoritarianism and those of insurrection were forever twinned, one of necessity giving birth to the other. Those who took action carried within them a pain and a rage that was cumulative. Historic humiliations, alive in shared memory, burned deep in the subconscious of those who, at long last, were driven to act—and there would *always* be those who were driven to act.

The question of political violence was one of the few that led Emma into a strategic quandary. Candace Falk, Goldman's devoted archivist, believes that Emma must have been present at many "backroom planning sessions" that considered taking militant action. No one will ever know to what extent she took part in these discussions, or what her vote would have been if violence *were* being proposed. All we do know is that however much she spoke against violence in public, she never failed to speak, write, and fund raise on behalf of anarchist comrades who had fallen afoul of the law on the charge of political terrorism. In this regard, all she ever had to do was invoke the image of Sasha Berkman and Homestead to feel herself on justified ground.

After Sasha's trial, Emma threw herself into working for the commutation of his sentence and persuaded almost every left-wing person and organization of note in New York to endorse the effort. Mass meetings were held, a committee was formed, fund raising begun. Working to attain Sasha's early release achieved the status of a holy grail for Emma. To even question the nobility of his act was to make oneself her instant enemy.

The absence of support from Johann Most came as a shock which she refused to sustain. It was true that Most no longer believed in attentat, but it was also true that he was hugely jealous of the place Berkman held in Goldman's affections, and when in his newspaper *Die Freiheit* he publicly condemned the

attack on Frick as an act of childish immaturity, his denunciation was seen by her as the grossest sort of betrayal. The second time he made this charge, in a public lecture in New York,
Goldman was in the audience and had come prepared to act.
When Most once again scorned Berkman, she leaped up onstage and struck him across the face with a whip; then she broke
the whip across her knee and threw the pieces at him. Years
later, she said, somewhat lamely, that she regretted the act—
"When you're twenty-three years old," she shrugged, "you
don't always act reasonably"—but it was the act not the regret
that contributed to the legend of Emma Goldman, firebrand
extraordinaire.

The fund-raising committee that Emma had formed on
Sasha's behalf began to meet weekly, and six months after the
attack on Frick, at one of these meetings, she met a man to
whom she quickly became attracted. The man was Ed Brady,
a tall, blond Austrian anarchist, just arrived in America after
having spent ten years in prison for the illegal publication of
anarchist literature. At the meeting Brady sat fidgeting with
matches. Flirtatiously, the twenty-three-year-old Goldman
took the matches out of the forty-year-old Brady's hand, saying, "Children shouldn't play with fire." He instantly replied,
"All right, grandmother, but you should know I'm a revolutionist; I love fire, don't you?" Within a matter of months, the two
had become lovers.

Ed Brady was also a life-changing event. To begin with, he
was the first man not simply to penetrate Emma but actually
to make love to her: a significant development on more than
one score. Emma suffered from what was then called an "in-
verted womb"—Candace Falk speculates that it was probably
a case of undiagnosed endometriosis, a condition of foreign
tissue growth that causes uterine pain and, almost always, in-
fertility—which meant, on the one hand, that she could not
easily become pregnant (a consequence she welcomed) and, on

the other, that she never had intercourse without excruciating difficulty. Up to this point she had been to bed only with inexperienced boys like Sasha or barbarians like Johann Most: men who supplied raw, unsatisfying excitement at a cost. With the gentle and worldly Ed, however, she experienced an intensity of sexual pleasure that mitigated the pain and opened her to a depth of sensual feeling that until now had eluded her. "It was in the arms of Ed that I learned for the first time the meaning of the great life-giving force. I understood its full beauty, and I eagerly drank its intoxicating joy and bliss."

She had begun her lifelong romance with the power of sexual infatuation. Very nearly, she likened the transporting emotion to anarchism itself: that's how significant she considered the sense of liberation that sexual ecstasy induces. This was an experience to be glorified all one's life. And why not? It was, indeed, the force of life from which, ultimately, she extracted the kind of insights upon which rested her intellectual contribution to world anarchism.

The estimable Brady was not only a tender and experienced lover, he was also a man of some cultivation. He introduced Goldman to world literature, giving her Goethe, Shakespeare, Rousseau, and Voltaire to read (later Wilde, Whitman, Ibsen, and Shaw), and—world-class autodidact that she proved to be—she was soon as enraptured by her reading as by her newly acquired intimacy with sensual joy. For these gifts alone she would have prized her connection with Brady. But he had even more to give her.

At this time she was working as a seamstress by day, speaking and demonstrating every chance she got (usually to and with Yiddish-speaking anarchist groups on the Lower East Side), and hanging out with Ed in the evenings at Justus Schwab's saloon on East 1st Street. Home to every kind of radical in New York—French Communards, Spanish and Italian refugees, Russian nihilists, German socialists, and anarchists from everywhere—the saloon took Ed and Emma as a couple to its heart; in Emma, in particular, Schwab himself found an adorable insurrectionist. "Emmachen," he would say regularly, "your head is not made for a hat, it is made for the rope. Just look at those soft curves. The rope would easily snuggle into them."

Life was good among the East Side radicals, but insular. Without quite knowing it, Emma was waiting for the next great adventure that would take her out into the larger world; this proved to be her arrest in August 1893 when she addressed the crowd of unemployed in Union Square and urged that if work were not given to them they were to demand bread, and if bread were not given, they were to take it.

Emma emerged from the jail on Blackwell's Island at the end of 1894 to discover that her status among New York progressives had undergone a sea change. Not only was Ed Brady waiting at the prison gates for her, so were a thousand other people up at the Thalia Theatre, where she was cheered as soon as she appeared on the stage. In her absence from the turbulent depression-era scene, she had become a radical celebrity. Oh, how delicious was that applause coming up over the footlights from those who lived in neighborhoods other than the ones occupied by the immigrant left! It held the promise of what she most hungered for, and had prepared for by learning English in prison: a place in the world beyond the Jewish ghetto.

It wasn't that Emma ever forgot she was a Jew or ever wished herself not a Jew. She spoke Yiddish fluently (it flavored her speech all her life), lived almost exclusively among Jewish radicals, and understood the historic plight of her people all too well. But devotion to Jewishness as an identity had never been compelling for her; that devotion was bound up with ritual beliefs that from earliest youth she had been unable to subscribe to. No sooner did she reach the age of reason than she saw herself as a freethinker and an internationalist. For Emma

Goldman, the Jewish Lower East Side had always been simply a staging ground.

Emma and Ed took an apartment together on East 11th Street and began a six-year relationship fraught, almost from the beginning, with the fallout from what quickly developed into a sharply divided notion of how they were to live. Like so many progressive men who fall in love with a New Woman precisely because she is a New Woman, Ed Brady, with all the goodwill in the world, was soon made unhappy by the very element that distinguished *his* New Woman: namely, her irrepressible activism. What he really wanted, it turned out, was a home and a family. Let's settle down and have children, he proposed. Emma's jaw dropped: Was he kidding? No, she told him, this was not her, never had been, never would be. Then she told him again—and yet again. For people who are infatuated but set on an internal collision course, this is the kind of conversation that is had many, many times before the meaning of its content exhausts the infatuation.

Meanwhile, Ed continued to act like the mensch he was. On Blackwell's Island, Emma had become a nurse's aide in the prison infirmary, and the work had given her a sense of purpose she had never before had in any day job. Now in 1895, Ed, in a gesture of large rather than narrow self-interest, insisted on sending her to Vienna for a degree in nursing and midwifery (to the Austrian Brady, only European training was valid). If he had daydreamed that nursing would make her see the domestic light, he would be in for a rude awakening. Goldman returned to the States a more articulated anarchist than she had been before she left.

Emma was twenty-six years old and wonderfully ripe for what lay before her. Turn-of-the-century Vienna was one of the most exciting cities in Europe—in fact, *the* most exciting. The excitement turned on the threat of social chaos that had been building all over the continent for the past forty years. After the 1848 uprisings, the failing aristocracies had been invaded but not replaced by a bourgeois liberalism that had proven too weak—that is, too self-absorbed—to achieve genuine democracy; *this* failure was sending history over the top. An enormous change in how ordinary people were coming to view the development of their own lives was in progress. This change would soon be called modernism.

For more than a century, belief in the supremacy of reason and moral self-control had held sway. Now, at the turn of the twentieth century, that belief began losing power; an indescribable restlessness was turning the Western world sharply away from the idea of rational man toward an ever-increasing interest in psychological man: that creature of feeling and instinct whom history had insisted on ignoring or denying. Political and economic success or failure was beginning to be assessed in terms of psychological satisfaction rather than Victorian morality. Such emotional concerns were, everywhere and especially in Vienna, swelling to crisis proportions. Cultivation of one's own psychic well-being became intensely fashionable among the middle classes . . . and one thing led inexorably to another.

In the course of curbing the power of those above it, bourgeois liberalism had released the energies of those below. Now, in the 1880s and 1890s, the middle class was being overtaken by rapidly expanding mass movements which in themselves seemed—and in the end were—menacing. Theodor Herzl, witnessing huge working-class demonstrations for social and political rights in Paris, described them as a form of group primitivism that filled him with dread. "They are like a great beast beginning to stretch its limbs," he wrote, "still only half conscious of its power."

This was an experience—unsettling in the extreme—that was being had everywhere in Europe, but nowhere more so than in Vienna. The writer Robert Musil remembered that in Vienna in those days "no one could quite distinguish between what was above and what was below, between what was moving forward and what backward." The city was shot through with an atmosphere divided in unequal, ever-shifting parts between apprehension and exhilaration. As every kind of authority—church, family, respectability itself—was being called into question, the most basic articles of social faith began to loosen their hold, and soon large numbers of people no longer knew what was expected of them.

This development allowed for the entertainment of thoughts and emotions hitherto unthinkable. Inevitably, the unthinkable led to the familiar growing strange, and—worse!— the strange familiar. It was then that the reliably static relation between society and the individual did an about-face, and an epic struggle was begun between the old-fashioned need for law and order and the newer-fashioned one for rights rights rights. Internal self-division—a sense of the culture being split down the middle—had itself made conscious the idea of an inner being; and a pressing hunger for emotional openness developed so rapidly that for a whole class of people it became a kind of hysteria that, as the historian Carl Schorske has it, was destined to transform "the promise of freedom into a nightmare of anxiety." The classic problem of the individual in a disintegrating society became conflated with the modernist revolt against Victorian moralism now gathering steam.

In Vienna a significant minority of artists and intellectuals, responsive to the underlying meaning of the social restlessness and now breakaways from the bourgeois culture that had supported them, determined, in the face of still vigorous middle-class disapproval, on a "newness" in dress, manners, the arts, and moral philosophy that would be expressive of the fractured state of social affairs. Thus, all over the Austrian capital the public culture displayed a mix of decadence and modernism whose effect only the word *heady* can begin to describe. Here was being born psychoanalysis as well as Nazism, transgressive art as well as retrograde nationalism, innovative architecture and social theory riddled with antisemitism (ah yes, of course! it was the Jews!)—all of it swirling around together in the air that one breathed daily.

Emma, registering the promise of what was to come rather than the threat of what was being lost, thrived on it all and avidly pursued the development of what she too now called her inner being. She read Nietzsche for the first time, saw Eleanora Duse act, heard Wagner's operas, and, most important, listened to Sigmund Freud lecture. Everyone she encountered in Vienna was memorable, but none more so than Freud, who had just begun formulating his seduction theory. In Emma Goldman—who could have imagined?—Freud had the perfect student. His concentration (as she heard it) on sexual repression as the root of all personal evil entered into her as a piece of immutable truth. The brilliance of his mind coupled with the earnestness of his manner gave her the feeling of "being led out of a dark cellar into broad daylight." For the first time, she wrote, "I grasped the full significance of sex repression and its effect on human thought and action." In time, although she continued to think of Freud as "a giant among pygmies," she came to consider psychoanalysis itself as "nothing but the old confessional," and her concentration on the idea of inner liberation as a prime political value is more easily traced to the twin influences of modernism and American individuation than to psychoanalytic thought. Nonetheless, the lived reality of Freud's world-changing insight about sexual repression and its extraordinary fallout continued to blossom in her, emotionally and intellectually, for the next forty years, becoming the interpretative touchstone for the political influences to which she was being exposed during that formative year.

On her way to Vienna, she had stopped in London, where

she had met Peter Kropotkin, the gentle theorist whose devotion to education rather than insurrection was now, in 1895, becoming the emblematic face of European anarchism. Like Bakunin, Kropotkin was also a child of the Russian aristocracy, but unlike Bakunin he was experienced as the most benign of spirits. "A man with a soul of that beautiful white Christ which seems coming out of Russia," as Oscar Wilde, with an uncharacteristic lack of irony, put it. Kropotkin's devotion to what he called the "scientifically proven" superiority of the impulse toward cooperation (as against Darwin's diametrically opposite claim for competition) had captured the moral imagination of many in Europe and had already begun to dominate the thinking of the anarchist movement in America. Goldman was only too happy to kneel at his intellectual feet.

Born in 1842 in Moscow, Peter Alexeyevich Kropotkin was the son of a Russian prince who owned huge tracts of land and the twelve hundred serfs who worked them. The boy grew up hating both the privilege and the slavery. Deeply troubled at having so much while so many had so little—who can ever predict what will drag at which heart—he yet remained a dutiful son, fulfilling his father's wish that he train at an elite military school and after graduation enter the army. Not wanting (ever) to see action, he chose to attach himself to a Siberian Cossack regiment, where he served as an aide-de-camp to the governor of a district in the Russian Far East. The work was administrative, and, soon bored, he volunteered to take charge of two successive geographical survey expeditions into the heart of Manchuria. These trips endued Kropotkin with a love of scientific exploration.

He quit the army, entered the university in Petersburg, and a few years later (now trained to understand what he was looking at) explored the glacial deposits of Finland and Sweden for the Russian Geographical Society. "What he observed," writes Paul Avrich, "led him to conclude that the theory of evolution, then the talk of intellectual Europe, had been seriously distorted by Darwin's followers. . . . Observations of animal and human life revealed few instances of internecine struggle among members of the same species. Far from ruthless competition, what he found was mutual aid." This "discovery" proved penetrating. On his way to becoming a professional student of natural science—and a man in possession of a privileged life— Kropotkin underwent a true emotional crisis, out of which he emerged a revolutionary. "What right had I to these higher joys," he brooded, "when . . . whatsoever I should spend to enable me to live in that world of higher emotions must needs be taken from the very mouths of those who grew the wheat and had not bread enough for their children?" These thoughts quickly achieved the status of an imperative. "No longer could he find peace in the work to which he had brought such gifts of observation and insight," notes Avrich. Far better that he should give up research and spend his life applying his bent for science to the social theory that placed him in the camp of the anarchists.

In 1888, Thomas Huxley, a Darwin disciple, published an influential essay, "The Struggle for Existence," in which he reiterated the now widely held conviction that competition *was* the major law of nature. An agitated Kropotkin replied at length. Then he replied a second, and a third, time. Nothing could shake his conviction that cooperation was at the heart of the survival of each species and the feature most responsible for evolutionary progress. Eventually the replies were gathered into Kropotkin's most famous book, *Mutual Aid: A Factor of Evolution*. Published in 1902, it contained the theory that became and remained the essence of his contribution to world anarchism.

What Kropotkin envisioned was a society of communes loosely bound in federation, depending for its very life on the principle of voluntary cooperation. Here, through the simplicity of direct democracy, people would live and work and flourish, each being compensated according to his or her need. Kropotkin understood that it would be a task to subdue the impulse of one human being to make instrumental use of another, and yet another task to nourish the impulse that would induce each one to see his or her own prosperity as bound up with the common good. But this, he was absolutely convinced, would constitute no real problem. As the first impulse was definitely the weaker of the two it would easily be overtaken by the second, which, in time, would grow organically out of the benign ground of the commune itself. It seems not to have occurred to him (as it does to no theorist) that irrational impulses, inappropriate desires, sheer human unpredictability might knock the whole scheme into a cocked hat.

Emma Goldman never resolved the conflict between her maturing belief in political change through education and her temperamental urge toward impassioned revolt. Thrilled by the sense of socialism as an evolutionary process—a transformation in thought and feeling that would grow itself from the inside out—she could readily see that the prospect of going forward through the accomplishment of inner change, rather than giving in to the explosive impatience that demanded an immediate end to government rule, would give anarchism the edge. Her attachment to the beloved Cause fired itself anew, and she returned to America fully prepared to pursue the life— the one she'd been born for—of the professional apostle of Kropotkin-style anarchism. But as it turned out, only rarely, in either her public appearances or her written work, would she invoke Kropotkin's utopian vision of communes of mutual aid; almost always it was her dramatic denunciation of the state that was remembered. Inevitably, temperament carried the day.

Settled again in New York, where she now began to support herself as a nurse and midwife (she made her living this way for many years), Emma was nonetheless, from this time on and for the better part of the next two decades, on the road at least six months out of every year, speaking and demonstrating on behalf of anarchism, and soon discovering that this was where she belonged. It was here—onstage and on the move, alone in the ever-changing crowd—that she felt most herself. The insight came as a revelation.

In the winter of 1898, in a column called "Letters from a Tour" (serialized in the German-language anarchist monthly *Sturmvogel*), Goldman observed that although it was not much fun to travel "when you have just enough to reach the next city, when you get something to eat from one person today (or perhaps not), and someone else tomorrow, when you have to sleep on the floor or in the family bed (without the father of the house, of course)"—still, it was "exactly such difficulties and unpleasant circumstances [that] lend a certain thrill to my travels. Perhaps because I am, (as a friend says), a born vagabond."

Speculating on the possible origin of this disposition, Goldman invoked—for one of the few times in her life—her Jewishness. Maybe it was the inherited rootlessness of the Jews that was now surfacing in her: the tradition of a people "always living on its wits and on the precipice of disaster," as Irving Howe once wrote, who preferred to keep moving rather than sit around waiting to be evicted (or worse). Maybe. But even she suspected that Jewish rootlessness was, at best, symbolic of a restlessness more driving, more complicated, more inexplicable than one people's cultural history alone could account for. The bottom line, she realized, was that "to stay in one place for months, years, or perhaps an entire life, always having to spend time with the same people . . . this disconsolately bleak monotony of every day life would fill me with horror."

Having always to spend time with the same people!

She had flashed on something crucial about herself that she was destined never to clarify, but to romanticize mercilessly.

The woman who spent her life in service to the idea of the individual was rubbed raw by steady, uninterrupted connection with any *one* of the many individuals who longed to count themselves her intimates. She lived in a mob scene, continually surrounded by a crowd of anarchist comrades, but something within her revolted against one or another of them coming too close for too long. Some abrasion of the spirit, there ever since she could remember, allowed her, paradoxically, to feel deeply for whole classes of people while disallowing specific attachments of any depth or duration to form. Except for the enduring bond with Sasha Berkman, it was through the Cause alone that she would ever know what George Sand called "the ripening harvest of long-cherished affection."

An emotional defensiveness stood between Emma Goldman and conventional intimacies, condemning her to a lifelong sense of aloneness that—again, paradoxically—she at one and the same time courted and longed to escape. Like most of us, instead of struggling to understand the conflict within she sought refuge in catharsis. Only one thing, she found, could alleviate the anxiety, and that was the illusory promise of short-term connection. For the ideal short take, it turned out, there was nothing like life on the road. In the decades ahead, Emma would often dramatize herself as a woman who had given up the stability of hearth and home for the peripatetic life to which the Cause had consigned her, but her love-hate relationship with her own loneliness was a more plausible explanation for the addictive traveling. And then, of course, the founding of *Mother Earth*, the anarchist magazine she called her love child, came to feed brilliantly into the self-division that drove her back on the road year after year after year.

Emma had always meant it when she said, "The most violent element in society is ignorance," and she had long dreamed of a magazine of her own that would provide a cornucopia of anarchist truths. The first issue of *Mother Earth*, billing itself as

"A Monthly Magazine Devoted to Social Science and Literature," appeared in March 1906. Its print run was three thousand, its cost ten cents, and on the cover appeared a drawing of a naked Adam and Eve (seen from the back) with a set of broken chains lying on the ground beside them. Goldman's initiating editorial announced that *Mother Earth* would be a forum for anarchism of every school and variety, covering freedom of speech, the labor movement, modern education, literature and the arts, birth control, free love, and prison reform, all without "sectarian favoritism"—and all with a view, editor Peter Glassgold tells us in his introduction to the anthology of *Mother Earth* pieces published in 2001, to celebrating anarchism's theoretical underpinnings, its heroes and martyrs, its uncompromising position on atheism, its relation to revolutionary violence.

In contrast to its great rival, *The Masses*, founded in 1912, *Mother Earth* was seriously intense. While *The Masses* covered much the same territory, it did so with humor, sexual sophistication, irreverence, and graphics galore; *Mother Earth* published sober, in-depth pieces that were long, analytic, and unadorned. In twelve years of publication there were only twenty-eight illustrations on its covers and inside the magazine only one political cartoon.

Nonetheless, during its short life—it ceased publication in 1917 when, at the height of America's first Red Scare, the post office refused to let it go through the mails—Emma's love child was a definite part of the radical literary scene. As a result of its nonsectarian policy, the magazine appealed to "socialists, single-taxers, militant Wobblies, social reformers, and even parlor liberals," and the people who wrote for it came to constitute a Who's Who of American radicalism in those years— Margaret Sanger, Floyd Dell, John Reed, Alexander Berkman, C. L. R. James, Voltairine de Cleyr, Errico Malatesta, Max Nettlau, Hippolyte Havel, and (from abroad and in translation) Peter Kropotkin, Lev Tolstoy, Maxim Gorki. The majority of the American contributions were articles with titles like "They Who Marry Do Ill," "The Place of Anarchism in Modern Thought," "Why Strikes Are Lost," "The Social Aspects of Birth Control," and "The Need of Translating Ideals into Life."

*Mother Earth* became a crucial center of Emma's life. The magazine was produced out of her New York apartment (Sasha Berkman was its editor between 1907 and 1915), and the people who helped run and support it became "family," swarming all over her place (first on East 13th Street and then up in East Harlem) morning, noon, and night. As the magazine was never self-supporting, it required the constant subsidy supplied by Emma's lecture tours and annual fund-raising masquerade balls, the last of which took place in 1915; announced as the Red Revel Ball, it drew eight hundred people (Emma came dressed as a nun and danced a waltz called "The Anarchist's Slide"). Thus, *Mother Earth* became both the reason and the excuse for much of Emma's traveling, thereby allowing her, legitimately, to mimic the practice of generations of men who explain their compulsive working lives by invoking the need to support "the family"—the one they prefer to experience in the abstract rather than the quotidian reality.

Ultimately, Emma came to discount the value of her thousand and one days and nights on the lecture circuit—"I came to see that oral propaganda is at best but a means of shaking people from their lethargy: it leaves no lasting impression"—but she was wrong to do so. The dynamism of the road, where she worked out her ideas, and encountered America, was the making of her. Between 1895 and 1917, as she crisscrossed the continent for weeks and months at a time, everything came magically together: the woman, the work, the period, all supremely well met.

The nineteenth century in America was a time when everyone in the country seemed to be out on the hustings, declaring, inventing, seducing: remaking themselves and the world each day anew through large, colorful presentations that were, for decades on end, the order of the day. Public speaking, "an overriding, astonishingly inclusive convention," as Garry Wills describes it in *Lincoln at Gettysburg*, became "a kind of performance art with great power over audiences." This was the American Chautauqua in its prime: a cultural free-for-all unequaled before or since. On the lecture circuit, you had polemicists and medicine men, opera singers and hypnotists, scam artists and humorists, as well as (during the years surrounding the Civil War) every major and minor speaker for abolition, temperance, universal suffrage, and moral transcendentalism, nearly every one of whom could deliver a two-hour performance saturated in image and metaphor, reaching back to the classics for the one and deep into the Bible for the other. Imagine hundreds of farmers, housewives, shopkeepers, lawyers, artisans, and schoolchildren crowding into makeshift meeting halls all over the country, gathered around bandstands, horse carts, or wooden platforms set up out in the open, or under the overhang of a railroad station, all of whom have traveled miles to hear an impassioned exhortation by the circuit speaker on behalf of abolition or Romantic poetry, temperance or Irish Home Rule, self-reliance or a cure for baldness, women's rights or justice in ancient Athens, and you will understand that "silver-tongued oratory" was there to feed hungers of the spirit that went otherwise unrelieved.

Lower East Side radicals, too, were developing their own considerable talents for oratory and exhortation. The anarchists, in particular, throughout the 1880s and 1890s held weekly forums that turned into marathon public debates where, as Irving Howe reports in *The World of Our Fathers*, "doctrine was expounded, the Almighty told off, and instruction offered in the social and natural sciences." All of which made the entire district rejoice. "When a debate was arranged, the audience could grow to several hundred or more [as] the immigrant world loved these gladiatorial exercises in oratory and dialectic." Recalling a debate between Saul Yanofsky, editor of the anarchist newspaper *Freie Arbeiter Stimme* (The Free Voice of Labor), and Louis Miller, a social democratic writer, an eyewitness writes, "Quotations pour out of Miller like burning lava from a volcano. He cites Marx and Bakunin, Kropotkin and Jules Guesde, Darwin and [Arabella] Buckley, Spencer and Hegel, Aristotle and Spinoza, until his opponent is utterly shattered. The hall resounds with applause. Miller has emerged triumphant."

In the 1890s Emma Goldman mastered a brand of leftwing rhetoric that competed successfully not only with that of the men in her own movement but with that of America at large: she could quote Marx and Hegel, and throw in Emerson, Charles Ingersoll, and Thoreau as well. Thousands of working-class people of every stripe and condition, longing for an explanation of why their lives were as they were, flocked to hear in Goldman's rich and resourceful flow of speech the words that would help them find a way out of the pain of their own ignorance. She was right to feel that people came to her lectures for amusement but wrong to think it was *only* for amusement. While these performances did deliver excitement and entertainment, quite often they also provided the fired-up beginnings of an autodidact's education. Looking at a typical lecture schedule handbill, circa 1915, announcing Goldman's appearance in Portland, Oregon, at the Scandinavian Socialist Hall, one can readily see why:

EMMA GOLDMAN
Who will deliver a Series of Lectures on Vital Subjects:

Sunday, August 1, 3 PM
THE PHILOSOPHY OF ANARCHISM

Sunday, August 1, 8 PM
THE "POWER" OF BILLY SUNDAY

Monday, August 2, 8 PM
MISCONCEPTIONS OF FREE LOVE

Tuesday, August 3, 8 PM
FRIEDRICH NIETZSCHE: The Intellectual
Storm Center of Europe

Wednesday, August 4, 8 PM
JEALOUSY: Its Cause and Possible Cure

Thursday, August 5, 8 PM
ANARCHISM AND LITERATURE

Friday, August 6, 8 PM
THE BIRTH CONTROL (Why and How Small
Families are Desirable)

Saturday, August 7, 8 PM
THE INTERMEDIATE SEX (A Discussion of
Homosexuality)

Sunday, August 8, 3 PM
WAR AND THE SACRED RIGHT OF PROPERTY

Sunday, August 8, 8 PM
VARIETY OR MONOGAMY—WHICH?

Particularly thrilling were the talks on jealousy, birth control, and homosexuality—especially the last; Emma Goldman explaining homosexuality from a public stage in 1915 was in itself almost actionable. The halls were packed, and the discussions that followed often memorable for the intellectual free-for-all they provoked. Of Emma Goldman it could have been said, as Ramsey MacDonald did of the IWW's Big Bill Haywood addressing the crowd in Hyde Park, that she "made them see things, and their hearts bounded to be up and doing."

For Emma herself, the practice was immensely fruitful. Each time she wrote a speech, delivered a lecture, addressed a crowd, she saw in her own argument for Anarchism with a capital "A" some new analogy or simile or metaphor that taught her how to think better about what she was thinking about. Speaking (always) of what this brand of socialism meant to her (and also always for two or three hours at a stretch), she delivered again and again—in talks on industrial capitalism or free love or the modern theater, on birth control or jealousy or political violence, on public education or striking miners or child development—an ever enlarging sense of the dramatic wholeness of private and public life.

The passion in Emma's speeches was driven by this extraordinary ability to call up the memory of her own experiences so effectively that those listening soon felt what she felt, hurt where she hurt, were insulted and outraged even as she was insulted and outraged—experienced, in fact, the shock of recognition that made them *see* the stunted quality of their lives as they had never seen it before. The brilliance of her speeches lay in their ability to link their humiliations to a description of hell—for you, and you, and *you*—under contemporary capitalism. The narrative thread running beneath the surface of any one of her thousands of public addresses concentrated relentlessly—and here is what America did for her—on the live issue of individuation: that which the individual human organism required in order to flourish; the very thing which, under the current system of social organization, it most definitely did not have.

All anarchists were agreed that the main evil of organized life was an economic one, but, Emma pointed out, they also maintained that "the solution of that evil can be brought about only through the consideration of *every* phase of life . . . the individual and the internal alongside the collective and external." In fact, it was the painful and bewildering relation between the individual and his or her surroundings that anarchism as a philosophy intended to address.

It was a tragedy for people to spend their lives doing what they hated doing: "Anarchism aims to strip labor of its deadening, dulling aspect, of its gloom and compulsion. It aims to make work an instrument of joy, of strength, of color, of real harmony, so that the poorest sort of a man should find in work both recreation and hope."

It was a tragedy to be deprived of "individual liberty and economic equality, the twin forces for the birth of what is fine and true in man," without which human growth is forever stunted or deformed. Anarchism would correct for these vital distortions.

It was more than a tragedy to remain in fearful thrall to the institutions that were meant to serve and to solace but only entrapped and imprisoned: "Anarchism stands for the liberation of the human mind from the dominion of religion; the liberation of the human body from the dominion of property; liberation from the shackles and restraint of government."

It was not that women and men did not need society; of course they did, people experience themselves only in relation to one another. The tragedy was that "the individual and society have waged a bloody battle for ages, each striving for supremacy because each was blind to the value and importance of the other." This dynamic had repeated itself throughout history because human beings, filled with primitive fears, had been taught for thousands of years that "man is a mere speck of dust dependent on blind, hidden forces ever ready to mock and taunt him." Thus had emerged the combined institutions of government and religion, insisting again and again, throughout the ages, that *man is nothing, the powers are everything.* Jehovah would tolerate man only "on condition of complete surrender." And what exactly was Jehovah's idea of complete surrender?

"Man can have all the glories of the earth, but he must not become conscious of himself."

Here, Emma would grow eloquent. Without consciousness, human life is animal life. Without consciousness there is no empathy. Without empathy, women and men transgress against one another. Transgression is deranging: it makes criminals of all who are not nimble enough to compete successfully. That was the worst of it. "What," she implored, "does society, as it exists today, know of the process of despair, the poverty, the horrors, the fearful struggle the human soul must pass on its way to crime and degradation?" And among those driven to break the law, how many understood the workings of their own situation sufficiently to think their way out of the trap?

Anarchism was an invaluable process of self-education whose aim was to develop the capacity for independent thinking that alone leads to freedom. Not an easy thing to acquire, independence of thought, as it is not a character trait but a human development whose salient characteristic is struggle; struggle that is, however, a blessing in disguise because "it is the *struggle* for, not so much the attainment, of liberty that develops all that is strongest, sturdiest, and finest in human character." And now at last she would get to where she had been going: the true enemy of every man, woman, and child is "the spirit of unquestioning obedience"—the very thing that contemporary education drills daily into our children. The question that should be occupying parents and educators alike today was whether children would be trained to social conformism or permitted "to grow from within" so that they might become expressive, independent-minded beings. As things stood now (here she might shake her head sadly), "The school for the child is what the prison is for the convict and the barracks for the soldier— a place where everything is being used to break the will." This was a situation *made* for the creation of enmity between institutions and individuals.

Anarchism, she would conclude, posited an organic unity of life, wherein the relation between the instincts of the individual and those of society need not be in conflict any more than were the heart and lungs of a human body: the individual being the heart, and society the lungs. While each needs the other, let us not forget that the *heart* is the essence of life, with the lungs in business to distribute "the element necessary to keep [that] essence—that is, the individual—pure and strong." It is the "individual instinct" that "is the thing of value in the world." In short: society is there to serve the individual, not the other way around. Why? Without a sense of one's own value, life is not worth living.

It was this sweep of narrative power that made Emma a star on the lecture circuit, and, the times being what they were, got her invited to speak not only to working-class audiences but to suburban women yearning for uplift, civil servants universalizing local politics, small-town theatergoers hungry for social significance, and, at the last, Greenwich Village bohemians whose modernist interests were trained on nothing less than full personal liberation. By 1910, she was mixing it up not only with the Philadelphia Ladies' Liberal League, the Kansas City Single Tax Society, the Seattle Social Science Club, and the Harvard Law Students Association but with the sophisticated participants of an evening at the socialite Mabel Dodge's lower Fifth Avenue salon.

Enter the Lyrical Left.

When the influence of European modernism crossed the Atlantic at the turn of the twentieth century, it made its first full stop in Greenwich Village, a raffish, irregular-shaped neighborhood at the bottom of Manhattan—close to both Union Square and the Lower East Side—whose name in time would become a worldwide synonym for bohemianism. Here in the 1890s began gathering a few hundred women and men of radical temperament for whom the idea of a revolution in cultural consciousness had gradually become a pressing need and then an extravagant demand. For the first but hardly the last time in American history a generation of artists, intellectuals, journalists, and social theorists arose for whom the words *free* and *new* had attained the status of holy writ. Many who only a short time ago had considered themselves simply independents in flight from the suffocation of bourgeois respectability now, at the turn of the century, saw themselves as artists in revolt. "Free speech, free thought, free love. New morals, new ideas, New Women"—these phrases had become crusading slogans among the women and men flocking to Greenwich Village, many of whose names are inscribed in the cultural histories of the time: Edna St. Vincent Millay, Floyd Dell, Alfred Stieglitz; Margaret Sanger, Eugene O'Neill, Isadora Duncan; Hutchins Hapgood, John Reed, Max and Crystal Eastman; Mabel Dodge, Louise Bryant, John Sloan; Margaret Anderson, Randolph Bourne, Walter Lippmann. A more unlikely collection of cultural bedfellows one could not readily imagine, but a great refusal was filling the air, one that made art and transgression and politics seem—as they always do in times of social rebellion—interchangeable agents of what was now being hungered for: a "regeneration of the just-before-dawn of a new day in American art and literature and living-of-life as well as in politics," as Max Eastman put it.

It was the spirit behind the enterprise that mattered: a spirit shared by all who were ready to experiment not only with art, sex, friendship, and marriage but with the disordered and the bizarre as well. *Experience* was king. To experience oneself through unimpeded sexual adventure, alarmingly bold conversation, extreme eccentricity of dress—to routinely declare oneself free to not marry or make a living, have children or vote—these became the extravagant conventions of downtown radicalism. It was as though in declaring yourself an instinctual being not only were you denying power to a bourgeois society terrified of direct experience; you were imposing original meaning on creation itself. History was a dead issue; yesterday was of no consequence; only the coming together of thought, feeling, and action mattered. An immense excitement surrounded the notion of refusing to accept that what had always been must always be. This excitement emboldened all who were drawn by it and made life seem an affair bursting with the emotional fearlessness usually associated only with extreme youth. And indeed: "The world was never so young as it is today," Walter Lippmann pronounced in 1912, "so impatient of old and crusty things."

Men like Lippmann, writing in *The New Republic*, or Randolph Bourne, in *Seven Arts*, or Max Eastman, in *The Masses*, were the intellectual gurus among the new radicals, explaining to the world and one another the values they thought they were influencing into existence. They all considered themselves Marxist sympathizers, but, remarkably, they advocated a theory of socialism that placed individual consciousness at the center of history. They did not read Marx, Spencer, and Darwin anywhere near as much as they read Nietzsche, Henri Bergson, and Freud, John Dewey and William James. As one of their followers explained, it was not the overthrow of the economic system that was wanted so much as "the will, the will to beauty, order, neighborliness." These were thinkers who prized James's trust that the "will to believe" was all that was necessary to achieve what Bergson called self-creation. *That* was the spirit to be placed at the center of all thought and action, political as well as artistic.

A major difference between European and American modernism was the concentration in America on a change in social consciousness as much through progressive politics as through the arts. By the early 1900s, Village artists and intellectuals were mingling with progressive reformers of every kind—suffragists, unionists, settlement workers. Artists and organizers alike worked to make a difference. They wrote, painted, and marched—for sexual liberation and collective bargaining, free speech and the eight-hour day, birth control and transgressive art. One of the most thrilling examples of this loosely knit coalition of like-minded spirits at work came about during the 1912 Lawrence textile strike (the Bread and Roses strike), one of the meanest battles in American labor history. With twenty thousand workers out on strike for ten dismal weeks, artists and intellectuals worked steadily with union organizers raising funds, housing children, running food stations, and sending in volunteer doctors in an effort to bring about something that resembled a victorious close.

In the 1910s Emma Goldman was made welcome in this world by many for whom the revolutionary activist embodied all that they themselves endorsed, and more. Not only were her causes (free speech, birth control, unlimited personal liberation) their causes; for people like Margaret Anderson, the intellectually sophisticated editor of the influential *Little Review*, Goldman herself was a figure of heroic stature. *She* was what it was all about. "Life takes on an intenser quality when she is there," Anderson declared, "something cosmic in the air, a feeling of worlds in the making." Anderson's imagination was literary and her interests existential—"Life is a glorious performance. In spite of the kind of 'part' one gets, everybody is given at least his chance to act"—but it was through exposure to Goldman's force of character that Anderson could propel herself imaginatively into the possibility of dramatic social change. Ah, those anarchists! "I never could listen to the socialists," she said. Socialism was just an explanation. But anarchism! "Anarchism, like all great things, is an announcement."

For a good ten years Emma Goldman moved easily among the downtown radicals, attending their parties, speaking at their rallies, reading their books, and going to their plays. "I have never known a people more rabid about art than the anarchists," Anderson enthused. "Anything and everything is art for them." That is, "anything containing an element of revolt." Goldman's ticket of admission to this world, the historian Christine Stansell is sure, was almost certainly her urgent "incitement to live fully in defiance of authoritarian structures," coupled with an ardent belief "in a self whose creative powers were unleashed by revolutionary ferment."

The welcome, however, was neither unqualified nor wholly flattering. Many were put off by the "Revolution 101" personality: Max Eastman found her unbearable, Mabel Dodge shrank from her. Yet Emma Goldman was too dramatic—too *exotic*—a figure to not make use of. She brought into a mainly theoretical conversation the excitement of street-smart activism. Mabel Dodge, the famous salonnière, loved revolutionary characters who performed themselves, so to speak: Big Bill Haywood, for instance, whose incendiary rhetoric made her shiver deliciously. Both Goldman and Haywood were invited often to Dodge's evenings, even though their presence in the room made her anxious: she always thought they were plotting *actual* revolution over there in the corner, whereas what she and her friends had in mind was revolution through self-*development*. On a number of scores, the relationship between Goldman and the moderns was a charade: the depth of her anarchism horrified some, the shallowness of her grasp of modern literature others. And then there was the issue which should have been a natural for them all: women's rights.

The clarity with which the new radicals saw women's rights as central to the cause of human solidarity was a genuine achievement. Women and men alike—Crystal Eastman and her brother Max, Ida Rauh and Floyd Dell, Margaret Anderson and Hutchins Hapgood—all endorsed suffrage for women, as well as sexual freedom, entry into the professions, recognition in the arts, release from domestic servitude. The issue of birth control was the one that struck the deepest nerve, and became the one around which Emma Goldman and the radicals *did* make brilliant common cause. Put her up on the stage of a lecture hall on behalf of birth control and, as the historian Linda Gordon writes, Goldman thrillingly "forged into a single ideology the many currents that mingled in American sex radicalism: anarchism, syndicalism, socialism; free lovers and utopians and feminists." When in 1916 she was arrested for distributing birth control materials, and Margaret Anderson said that Emma Goldman was going to jail for telling women that they "need not always keep their mouths shut and their wombs open," the remark gratified the astonishing range of politically minded people to whom Gordon refers.

Nonetheless, the misunderstandings between Goldman and the feminists were monumental. Neither ever grasped fully what the other was about. Goldman never understood that the feminists *needed* legal reform; the feminists never understood that she *needed* the law abolished.

Emma Goldman was not a feminist; she was a sexual radical, which made her a supporter of birth control and a defender of sex without marriage but not a proponent of women's rights as that term is generally understood. Her writings on the subject are eye-opening and jaw-dropping. She did not oppose suffrage, but she reviled the suffrage movement; she was all for personal emancipation, but she scorned women in the professions; she thought women should work, but she pronounced motherhood the most important thing in a woman's life; her contempt for the strong-willed modern woman who had lost the "sacred desire" for love and motherhood was boundless. D. H. Lawrence could not have improved on Goldman's diatribes against the sterility of the modern woman's life. For many feminists of her own time—and certainly for one of ours—these writings represent an exasperating and, yes, painful muddle.

The generation of Elizabeth Cady Stanton and Susan B. Anthony, as Goldman saw it, was noble—*those* women were visionaries. But the humorless, one-issue suffragists of her own time were unworthy successors to the great figures of the past. In a piece on woman suffrage she derides the obsessiveness of the suffragists, who act as though they think suffrage will deliver women from all the evils of life. What nonsense! "Woman's demand for equal suffrage is based largely on the contention that woman must have the equal right in all affairs of society." Suffrage however, is not a right, lectures Goldman the anarchist, it is an imposition. "Yet woman clamors for that 'golden opportunity' that has wrought so much misery in the world, and robbed man of his integrity and self-reliance." What a shame it all is, because this obsession with emancipation "has made of the modern woman an artificial being . . . robbed her of the fountain springs of that happiness which is so essential to her" (namely, love and motherhood). Bad enough for working-class women, this ignorant call for independence, but even worse for the women "in the more cultured professional walks of life—teachers, physicians, lawyers, engineers, etc.— who have to make a dignified, proper appearance, while the inner life is growing empty and dead."

If only she, Goldman, could make them see: "Until woman has learned to . . . listen to the voice of her nature, whether it calls for life's greatest treasure, love, love for a man, or her most glorious privilege, the right to give birth to a child, she cannot call herself emancipated. How many emancipated women are brave enough to acknowledge that the voice of love is calling, wildly beating against their breasts, demanding to be heard, to be satisfied. . . . The right to vote, or equal civil rights, may be good demands, but true emancipation begins neither at the polls nor in the courts. It begins in woman's soul. . . . The demand for equal rights in every vocation of life is just and fair; but, after all, the most vital right is the right to love and be loved."

As an anarchist Goldman, of course, opposed the institution of marriage; but while feminists railed against marriage primarily because the contract meant civil death for women (as well as the life sentence that marriage without friendship or intimacy imposed), for Goldman it was all about the death of sexual passion. The concept of love and marriage as synonymous, as the popular notion had it, was laughable. Au contraire: love and marriage are antagonistic. Not only does marriage kill love, it inflames that most reprehensible of emotions, jealousy. The problem, you see, is the contract. In a piece published as a pamphlet in 1911 and devoted to the subject of jealousy, she analyzes the situation as follows:

"In the past, when men and women intermingled freely without interference of law and morality, there could be no jealousy, because the latter rests upon the assumption that a certain man has an exclusive sex monopoly over a certain woman and *vice-versa.*" It is only nowadays, when men and women consider each other *property*, that we have jealousy, an emotion unrelated to the love that is given freely and received freely: "Two people bound by inner harmony and oneness are not afraid [of impairing] their mutual confidence and security if one or the other has outside attractions, nor will their relations [ever] end in vile enmity." Even if love fails, jealousy between people who are free agents is impossible: "Anguish over the loss of love or a non-reciprocated love among people who are capable of high and fine thoughts will never make a person coarse. Those who are sensitive and fine have only to ask themselves whether they can tolerate any obligatory relation, and an emphatic *no* would be the reply."

And there's an end of the matter. Abolish contractual love (marriage), and you do away not only with jealousy but with all instances of emotional delinquency. This is an article of faith applicable to relationships between parents and children as well as between lovers: "Few children [born] in wedlock enjoy the care, the protection, the devotion free motherhood is capable of bestowing. . . . So long as love begets life no child is deserted, or hungry, or famished for the want of affection."

These words were written in a time when unwed pregnancy induced the kind of social ostracism meted out to lepers; and girls and women of every class, in every part of the world, were smothering their illegitimate babies at birth. Nonetheless, to work for legal reform was for Goldman a distortion of woman's inherently heroic task: "Her development, her freedom, her independence, must come from and through herself. First by asserting herself as a personality, and not as a sex commodity. Second by refusing the right to anyone over her body; by refusing to bear children unless she wants them; by refusing to be a servant to God, the State, society, the husband, the family . . . freeing herself from the fear of public opinion and public condemnation. Only that, and not the ballot, will set woman free, will make her a force hitherto unknown in the world, a force for real love, for peace, harmony, a force of divine fire, of life-giving, a creator of free men and women."

Such sentiments were far better suited to the feminism of 1970, when essentialist notions of woman's "real" nature were being argued more equably by feminists still struggling for equality of citizenship—than to that of 1910, when women not only did not have the vote; once they married they had no legal existence at all: they could not keep their own money or property, could not decide on their children's—much less their own!—education, could not refuse their husbands sexual congress, could not sue for divorce.

The problem was, indeed, "love"—a problem peculiar among anarchists to Emma Goldman, and one that led her into an irony of historic proportions. On the one hand, it was love free of legal obligation that made her think more deeply about how stifled were the lives of women in particular. In fact, the connection she made between sanctioned love and the age-old subordination of women became the basis of Goldman's intellectual originality. When she wrote that Woman "must assert herself a personality, and not a sex commodity. . . must refuse to be a servant to God, the State, society, the husband, the family," she was doing for anarchism what Friedrich Engels did for Marxism when he equated the structure of the family with that of capitalism: both were making the personal political. Sexual freedom for women was the metaphor through which Goldman could see straight down to the center of anarchism for the individual. That is what love as a theory-making experience did for Emma Goldman. On the other hand, love on the ground—love as she actually experienced it, as opposed to how she idealized it—that was another matter.

For Emma, erotic love—"the strongest and deepest element in all life, the harbinger of hope, of joy, of ecstasy; the defier of all laws, of all conventions; the freest, the most powerful molder of human destiny"—was the quintessential experience; in fact, for Emma the experience was mythic. In this respect she was at one with the moderns. For them, as for Emma, free love was the objective correlative to visionary politics. Unmarried sexual radicals, in those years, thought they were making the revolution every time they went to bed with one another. To practice the fulfillment of one's own much-idealized desires was to declare a bold, risk-taking commitment to the "new" consciousness.

What no one understood (neither the Greenwich Village moderns nor Emma) was that in free love they had a tiger by the tail. Between the ardor of revolutionary rhetoric and the dictates of flesh-and-blood reality—that is, the simplicity of ideology up against the complication of emotional need—lay a no-man's-land of untested conviction. Here, for example, Emma declares with magnificent certainty that motherhood is the most important thing in a woman's life, and yet she herself adamantly refused to have children; here the men among the moderns loudly announced their allegiance to woman's rights and turned a blind eye to the sexism practiced daily in their own lives; here one anarchist after another spouted the rhetoric of violence, while each in turn quaked at the thought of personally throwing the bomb. This is the gap, so to speak, between practice and theory: the one into which most of us fall most of the time. The interesting thing about this gap is what happens once one is faced with the discrepancy between the real and the ideal. Is one then fortified by the insight or demoralized by it? Does one take in the contradiction or expel it from one's consciousness? Does ideology temper itself—or redouble its insistence? Either way, the response is of the utmost consequence.

The turn-of-the-century moderns were admirable in that many of them, when forced to look squarely at things as they were, chose to honor the evidence of their senses, even though that inevitably meant the beginning of the end, not necessarily of their ideals but certainly of their rhetoric. To see oneself in the gap was, almost always, to lose heart for spouting grand, unalloyed certainties.

On the other hand, it takes a certain kind of mad courage to reject the claim of experience as superior to that of idealism, and to go on insisting, against all odds, that ultimately the ideal *will* work because it *must* work, because it is not acceptable that it *not* work. This is the courage of the born refusenik, who, any day of the week, will discard defeatist reality in favor of the elevating ideal.

Emma's lifelong devotion to sexual radicalism as an article of faith—ongoing and unchanged in the face of one failed passion after another—is perhaps the single most important reflection of what her life as a professional revolutionary signifies. However many times the star in the starlike quality of the grand passion flared, fizzled, and turned to ash, Emma insisted that the star was fixed and that the next time it came into view you, too, would see that it was fixed. This she declared at the

end of her life as well as in the middle, imprinted as she permanently was by the significance of a sensation she invariably
mistook for an epiphany.

Enter Ben Reitman.

"He arrived in the afternoon, an exotic, picturesque figure
with a large black cowboy hat, flowing silk tie, and huge cane
. . . a tall man with a finely shaped head, covered with a mass
of black curly hair, which evidently had not been washed for
some time. His eyes were brown, large, and dreamy. His lips,
disclosing beautiful teeth when he smiled, were full and passionate. He looked a handsome brute. His hands, narrow and
white, exerted a peculiar fascination. His finger-nails, like his
hair, seemed to be on strike against soap and brush. I could not
take my eyes off his hands. A strange charm seemed to emanate
from them, caressing and stirring."

All her life, Emma remembered their first time together as
one of unearthly excitement, so shocked was she by the force of
sexual passion that overtook her.

Ben Reitman was ten years younger than Emma (he was
twenty-nine when they met, she thirty-nine). Born in the Mid-
west, dragged up by a deserted, impoverished mother, street-
wise by the age of ten, he ran away in early youth, rode the rails,
lived in hobo camps, and came to feel deeply at one with an
underclass population of vagrants, activists, whores, and criminals. In time he returned to Chicago, went to medical school,
and became the Hobo Doctor—later known as the Clap Doctor—to the raucous, unlettered, semi-lawless dropouts among
whom he felt most himself, developing a lifelong interest in
rescuing the homeless from pariah status by educating them to
"confront the society that was crushing [them] underfoot." In
1907 he opened his Hobo College in Chicago, one of the many
so-called migratory workers' universities of the time, and led
a historic march of the hobo unemployed. Flamboyant, impul-

sive, intellectually raw, Reitman was a dynamite promoter and organizer, an instinctive enemy of capitalism, and a pathological womanizer.

They met in March 1908 when Emma showed up in Chicago to speak, and the hall that had been arranged for — as happened often when she came to speak — was suddenly made unavailable, as was every other hall in town. In the midst of the confusion that overtook the situation, Ben Reitman walked in, offered her the Hobo College for the evening, and also offered to promote the event. The result: an overflow crowd and articles in the Chicago papers on Emma Goldman and the question of free speech.

She slept with him that same night, and the sex, she later said, was like nothing she had ever before experienced. Although she left Chicago as planned (she *was* on tour), in Minneapolis she dreamed "that Ben was bending over me, his face close to mine, his hands on my chest" and when she woke up, she sent for him. By June of that year, Emma and Ben had been together on the road for four months — he had quickly become her promoter and manager — and she was addicted to him. His primitive qualities, she said, had robbed her of her reason, had in fact aroused the primitive in her. She wanted to devour him, "yes, put my teeth into your flesh and make you groan like a wounded animal."

Many artists and intellectuals were made gaga by liberated love in these years, and in this department Emma and Ben more than held their own. Feeling deliciously subversive, they created a private language of code words — Rebecca West and H. G. Wells, among others, did the same — with which to write each other letters of erotic intensity that heightened the drama in which they felt themselves engaged. In these letters, Emma's vagina is her treasure-box (t-b), Ben's penis his Willie (W), her breasts M (for Mont Blanc and Monts Jura). They both talked baby-talk porn but Emma, especially, was outrageous: "I want my sweetheart, Willie boy, I want to give him the t-b, she is simply starved and will swallow him alive when she gets hold of him. . . . Come hold me, hobo dear, let me nestle up, let me . . . run a red hot velvety tongue over W and the bushes. . . . put my face to W and drink myself to sleep." Entranced by oral sex, she repeatedly wants to suck the head of his "fountain of life," which stands over her "like a mighty specter." Or alternately, "I press you to my body close with my hot burning legs. I embrace your precious head." One feverish morning in 1910 she wrote, "Its five am. Even if I am tired and weary and love hungry for my no account lover, I should show him [W] some things if he were here. Come close and see two actually big Ms and a little bright-eyed t-b."

Ben as well as Emma, it seemed, had often to take a calming bath after reading or writing one of these letters—a practice that went on, literally, for years.

Almost everyone Emma knew was put off by Ben Reitman: Sasha Berkman loathed him. Max Eastman refused to share a platform with him. Margaret Anderson maintained that "he wasn't so bad if you could drop all your ideas as to how human beings should look and act." Roger Baldwin (future founder of the American Civil Liberties Union) pronounced him "a terrible man, overbearing, arrogant, possessive . . . never faithful to Emma for a minute." But sexual infatuation is a force of formidable proportions, a projection of the senses at whose heart lies a psychological nostalgia that goes so deep it feels primeval; under its influence one "sees" something of oneself in the beloved that compels against all reason. While the infatuation endures it exerts the strength of Samson. And so it was with Emma and Ben. Each recognized something in the other—perhaps it was the emotional hobo in themselves—and that recognition, once eroticized, had the power to seal them into a blend of pain and euphoria that would sustain the most astonishing amount of humiliation before it ran its course.

They traveled together six months out of the year, with Ben arranging meetings, hiring halls, selling anarchist literature at Emma's talks, and warming up the audience by enjoining members to "take a chance, invest a nickel" (that is, buy a pamphlet) before the "big show" began. Mortified by the circus into which he turned her events, Emma nonetheless had to tip her hat to the thing in him that most excited her—that reckless "American swagger"—and she certainly had to acknowledge the immense value of what his love of publicity and showmanship could accomplish.

A month after they met she was already experiencing the excitement of being one half of a notorious couple. No sooner did they get off the train in San Francisco than they were surrounded by cops and reporters, and the San Francisco *Examiner* was screaming, "EMMA GOLDMAN IS ST. FRANCIS GUEST. ANARCHIST ARRIVES FROM SACRAMENTO WITH 'KING OF TRAMPS' AND DETECTIVES." Why detectives? Because the rumor had it that Red Emma had come to blow up the naval fleet in the San Francisco harbor. As a result, "meetings," Emma later wrote, "were veritable encampments. For blocks the streets were lined with police in autos, on horseback, and on foot. Inside the hall were heavy police guards, the platform surrounded by officers. Naturally this array of uniformed men advertised our meetings far beyond our expectations." Ben was quick to exploit the situation: audiences were swollen by the curious and the sensation seeking as well as the anarchist faithful.

Another few months and Emma was bringing in 1,500 to 2,000 people a night in towns and cities all over the country. In 1910 alone, she lectured 120 times in 37 cities in 25 states to audiences before whom anarchism had never been spoken of; 25,000 paid admission. In 1911 in Lincoln, Nebraska, a tremendous welcome from the most conservative of law student associations. In 1912, in Butte, Montana: "fifteen hundred people glued to the [open-air] spot for nearly two hours, with an attentiveness and earnestness I have rarely found in a hall." In 1915: "six cities, twenty meetings, 7,000 people, all crowded into three weeks." It was giddy-making—"What a panorama life is for him who lives intensely and dangerously. . . . Such a life leaves no room for monotony." And it was, she acknowledged, the skill and devotion of Ben Reitman that had made it all happen. These were certainly the best years of her life: she was famous, she was influential, she was on the move, doing a star turn every evening and making love all night.

There was just one small fly in the ointment. Ben Reitman was more than a compulsive womanizer; he suffered from what can only be called satyriasis. There was not a moment of his waking life—wherever he was, whatever he was doing, with Emma around or Emma away—that he wasn't scheming to get some woman into bed. Almost every night on the road, while Emma was up on a platform speaking, Ben would wander off with a pickup, making sure most (but not all) of the time to be back in the hall before she was off the stage.

Emma was astonished. Free love, for her, had definite characteristics: great passion was one of them, a quick fuck was not, much less a million quick fucks. Soon she was appalled to see herself doing what she had repeatedly said a free agent could never do. "The same woman," observes Candace Falk, "who affirmed in her coast to coast lecture tours that 'whether love last but one brief span of time or for eternity, it is the only creative, inspiring, elevating basis for a new race, a new world' now found herself in the depths of the uninspiring emotions of jealousy and self-doubt."

Every time she discovered Ben with another woman she felt as though she were losing her mind. "Hobo, I am raving," she wrote him, "I am feverish, I am ill with anxiety. . . . Oh, I shall commit violence. I must stop, I must pull myself together." But she couldn't. Once when, right before her eyes, Ben had gone off for a one-night stand, she wrote, "The woman you have awakened into frantic, savage, hungry life, recoils from you, feels outraged because you have thrust her aside for a moment's fancy, because you have outraged her sacred shrine, that tent, oh God, where passion held its glorious maddening feast. Oh, it is horrible, horrible! . . . The agony that our love has not saved us from the same coarse vulgar scenes of the ordinary has completely paralyzed me." Another time, another woman, she wrote, "Now all is dark, I cannot see, nothing is left of life. . . . I am so chilled and pained, I am struggling, the bitterest struggle of my life and if I succeed I fear I shall never be able to see you again. Yet, if I fail, I shall stand condemned before the bar of my own reason." Emotional tumult, baby-talk porn, the melodrama of self-abasement, these were the major characteristics of an affair that took ten years to wear itself out.

Over and over again Emma said that she could not accept the chaos and humiliation that went with loving Ben—no, no, she could not, she would not, such passivity undermined every ability she had to respect herself—and over and over again she caved. Before the drama of such compulsion, analysis paled. "Sex," she marveled in a letter to her beloved niece Stella, "is like a double-edged sword. It raises us to sublime heights and thrusts us into the lowest depths." As though commenting on immutable law, she also observed that "what people will do to each other in their intimate relations they would never do to their friends." This was the moment when she should have seen herself caught in the gap between practice and theory—and found the strength to either accept the situation as it was, or end the affair. But that moment never came. Living inside a cauldron of high-voltage emotion, with soul-destroying depression alternating regularly with convulsive desire, turned her on.

Ben Reitman is always written of as though he was Emma's one and only grand passion. As it turned out, he was a template upon which became inscribed a number of grand-passion knockoffs, so to speak, many of which, albeit compressed into a period of months rather than years, bear a startling resemblance to the original.

Seven years after parting from Ben—seven years that included deportation from America, near expulsion from the Soviet Union, an exiled existence in Europe, with many small "obsessions" (her word for affairs) along the way—Emma would seize another opportunity for renewed passion when it presented itself, and perform in exactly the same high register she had done with Ben.

Leon Malmed, a fellow-traveling anarchist, twelve years her junior, whom Emma met when on tour in 1906, is now, twenty years later, a married delicatessen-store owner in Albany who has helped raise funds to bring Emma, long exiled from the United States, to Canada on a lecture tour. She has always thought of him as a good soul—loyal, hard-working, rank and file—but now, fifty-seven years old and famished for a renewal of both anarchism and love, she explodes into wild feeling: "Dearest boy, what greater love is there than one which binds two people in a great ideal? And ours is that, is it not?" The unprepared Malmed never knows what hit him.

In Montreal, at the start of her tour and before they even consummate their attraction, Emma tells Leon that their "relationship" (she has already moved into a relationship) has made her forget that she was "a stranger among strangers," and has filled her with "a mad longing for all that was denied me for so many years." Leon nods eagerly, but really is not too sure he knows what's going on. In any event, he's gotta get back to the store in Albany—he'll call her. When he does, Emma goes over the top: "I got so worked up, I am shaking from head to my feet, hearing your voice so unexpectedly aroused me to a wild pitch and lifted the depression like a thunderstorm. I am myself amazed at this new terrific force that you helped to unloose in my soul. All these many years I had the deepest affection for you as a devoted friend and comrade." But now, "all the suppressed elemental forces have broken loose in me, [and] I hold you pressed to my throbbing heart."

Inevitably, things become difficult with Leon—shopkeeper first, anarchist second, lover third—and Emma, who has prolonged her stay in Canada on his account, is getting frustrated. When Leon buys a second store in Albany, and thus has even less time for her, her frustration rises to an incendiary pitch, and she refuses to sleep with him the next time he does come to see her. She writes to explain why: "No girl of 18 waits for the arrival of her love as I wait for yours. My imagination is aflame with a thousand wild fancies. But the moment you are before me I see what you have left behind, like a shadow, it follows you. I hear you talk of nothing else but Albany and all my visions are wiped out, my heart contracts and I have a feeling as if someone would hold me by the throat. I am telling you this so you may understand why I am unable to respond to what my soul craves so violently." The affair ends very badly indeed.

Eight years later (she's now sixty-five years old), after years of lobbying by influential friends, she is granted a ninety-day legal visit to the United States, and meets Frank Heiner after one of her lectures in Chicago. Frank, a former osteopath, is thirty-six, married, and blind. He also has the emotional maturity of a twelve-year-old, admitting openly that he is in love with a fantasy of Emma he has carried around with him for years. She responds instantly, and before anyone knows what's happening is once more head over heels in love. The role of the "other woman" is not one she would have chosen—especially not with a blind man whose wife must read him her letters—but, hey, here we are.

After her three months in the United States are up, Frank

meets her in Toronto, and they shack up in a hotel room for two delirious weeks. Emma is beside herself with hope and happiness. All her previous relationships, she now says, pale before this one. To Stella she writes, "It is strange, isn't it, dearest mine, that I should wake up at 65 to the realization that with all the men I had known intimately my love had never [before] been fulfilled." Wha-a-t?

Eventually she has to book passage back to Europe (she is now living in France). On the ship, she realizes that she has made a terrible mistake. She should have remained in Canada. Once again, she's tearing her hair and feeling as though she were going mad:

> Oh my Frank, it was insanity to think I could enjoy life separated from you by thousands of miles. . . . It is impossible to endure. . . . I am alone, without you I am alone as never in my life have felt. . . . [I]t was madness, madness to have gone away. . . . But for our two weeks in Toronto I might not have missed you so frightfully. Since then I have tried desperately to eliminate you from my being. I have reasoned with myself that we might be good comrades and friends, and that I should learn to content myself with that. But the more I reason, the more every nerve cried out for you, your inspiring presence, your wild passion, your magic touch, your beautifully understanding Mind. Why did you have to bewitch me so, take possession of all my thoughts . . . an earthquake that shattered all my reserves. . . . It was the most spontaneous, most elemental, most overpowering event in my life. Just the same I should have fought against it. . . . I have nothing now, [certainly not what] I crave most. . . . I dream about you night after night . . . weary with the heart hunger for your presence and your embrace. . . . I see nothing before me but space and time. . . . Why should this have happened at this time in my life. . . . I hold you close to my longing and aching heart. With love, deep and intense passionate love.

In time, Frank Heiner writes to reveal his dirty little secret: she is not the first older woman "physically above the average weight" whom he has loved; in fact, all his life he has had an obsessive desire to bury himself in the flesh of a mother figure. For a moment she is crushed—it's the "physically above the average weight" that gets to her—but soon Frank will take his place in the pantheon of Great Loves Denied that would be idealized in memory (and in print).

In her memoir, musing on "the forces at work" that seemed bent on refusing her stability in love, she concluded: "The stars could not be climbed by one rooted in a clod of earth. If one soared high, could he hope to dwell for long in the absorbing depths of passion and love? Like all who had paid for their faith, I too would have to face the inevitable. Occasional snatches of love; nothing permanent in my life except my ideal."

Emma announced repeatedly that if reality began to usurp the ideal, she would ditch reality in less than a second. She would *never* opt for living without a life- (or world-) saving ideal to believe in—not only to believe in, to worship. Every weakness or perversity in her own and everyone else's behavior, every irrationality, every displaced anger, every mean insecurity she attributed to external forces. In and of itself, she insisted, our nature is benign. More than benign. In "sacred desire" she saw the majesty of something in the human condition that she, as an anarchist, was pledged to redeem. The renewal of love aroused in her the sense of paradise gained and lost that haunted every anarchist's fundamental conviction that the world as it is resembles a forfeiture of humankind's original nobility. To feel transformed by sexual passion was to be in touch with the primeval at the heart of her politics.

This belief in the mythic power of erotic love was, a hundred years ago, shared by the whole of Western culture. Poets and intellectuals, businessmen and philosophers, teachers and lawyers saw in its pursuit a metaphor for liberation of the spirit at the highest level. To *know* love was to penetrate the mysteries of the human condition, to see with radiant clarity the meaning of life and the world, not as it is but as it could be.

Emma Goldman's anarchism burned with original power for a good fifty years because she never abandoned her devotion to Love with a capital "L."

# Part III

---◆◆◆◆◆---

## *Exile*

As for my fame and your infame, I would be
willing to exchange a good deal of mine for a bit
of yours. It is not hard to write what one feels as
truth. It is damned hard to live it.

—EUGENE O'NEILL TO ALEXANDER BERKMAN,
January 29, 1927

THE 1917 sedition trial of Emma Goldman and Alexander Berkman, which ended with a two-year prison term for each, followed by deportation, ranks among the more egregious events in the history of political repression in the United States masquerading as protection of the democracy. For thousands of Americans, it was the distortion of the national ideal that hurt the most. "Who that heard it," the radical journalist John Reed wrote, "will ever forget the feeling of despair he experienced when Judge Mayer charged the jury, 'This is not a question of free speech, for free speech is guaranteed under the Constitution . . . but free speech does not mean license.'" Margaret Anderson assured her readers that Reed's despair was not confined to radicals: "One newspaper reporter told me that this trial was making a good Anarchist of him; a university professor who came to all the hearings told me that he had always had a respect for the law until now; one of the biggest lawyers in the city said the prosecution hadn't a leg to stand on; a recognized intellectual remarked that 'Russia has never had cause for such rebellion as we are now facing.'"

On the eve of the First World War the decades-long struggle between American radicals and vigilante patriotism reached fever pitch. In a state of near hysteria, the government enacted one repressive law after another, each one more abusive of guaranteed civil rights than the last. First came the May 1917 Selective Service Act, and with it the sudden activation of a conspiracy law already in place that made it a felony to object to conscription. A month later the Espionage Act was passed and within a year the equally infamous Sedition Act of 1918, both of which broadly defined sedition to include any sort of open dissent from government policy. These laws carried the threat of penalties of up to ten thousand dollars in fines and twenty years in prison and were, in effect, designed to muffle any and all criticism of the war or the government's execution of it. Under these laws, from 1917 to 1921—one of the most politically ignominious periods in American history—between four and ten thousand people were arrested on charges of disloyalty; ultimately, less than six hundred of these charges were upheld in court.

Throughout the summer and fall of 1917 government suppression of antiwar dissent escalated so swiftly and so recklessly that civil libertarian heads were swimming. Then in October, when the Bolsheviks took power in Russia, both state and federal governments "turned the country into a lunatic asylum" (as Emma put it), with wholesale raids and arrests and sentences of incredible severity being carried out daily.

The leadership of the IWW (some 165 strong) was arrested in its entirety after the organization's meetings had been banned or broken up, its halls raided and wrecked, its newspaper seized and denied mailing privileges. Bill Haywood was given twenty years for conspiring to hinder the draft, and more than a hundred other Wobblies got one to ten. (Haywood skipped bail and made his way to the Soviet Union, where he remained for the rest of his life.)

Rose Pastor Stokes, a well-known labor organizer, was given a prison sentence of ten years for saying in a letter to the *Kansas City Star* that "no government which is for the profiteers can also be for the people, and I am for the people while the government is for the profiteers."

A group of young anarchists in New York were arrested for printing a protest against American intervention in the Russian Revolution; they drew sentences of as high as fifteen years each.

The socialist Eugene Debs was sentenced to ten years in prison simply for speaking out against the Espionage Act; his colleague and comrade Kate Richards O'Hare was given five years for an antiwar speech she made in North Dakota.

The September 1917 issue of *The Masses* was confiscated and its editorial board indicted on charges of undermining the war effort; the legal action eventually forced the magazine to cease publication.

And all of this was happening on the basis of opinion, written or spoken—but opinion only. As the cultural critic Randolph Bourne said that year, "In a time of faith skepticism is the most intolerable of insults."

"It was evident to all of us in the *Mother Earth* group," Ben Reitman wrote years later, "that the jail and maybe the gallows were before us. Many took cover. Some found safety in joining the Army, others in getting married, others in going to Mexico, and still others by changing their names and their nationalities. Not so with Emma Goldman and Alexander Berkman. They became more revolutionary, more violent, and less compromising."

One of the reasons that Goldman and Berkman became, as Reitman put it, even more daring than they had been before was the alarm and contempt they felt in the face of the near total cave-in of the liberal intelligentsia, most of whom turned "patriotic" overnight. They were not alone in feeling this contempt—Randolph Bourne wrote a blistering piece called "The War and the Intellectuals" echoing the sentiment—but they were almost alone in acting on it. A secondary prod for action on Emma's part was her memory of another protest against another exclusionary act passed when another shameful alarm over dissenters had ruled the land—and that time, too, liberals and progressives had been shocked and outraged but remained silent, while she had been among the courageously incensed few to take the kind of action that might fail in the moment but in the long run would keep alive the issue of free speech.

Early in 1903—still reeling from the assassination of William McKinley two years earlier—Congress had passed the Anarchist Exclusion Act. In October of that year, the English anarchist John Turner was arrested after he had spoken at the Murray Hill Lyceum in New York City; when immigration officers found a copy of the anarchist newspaper *Free Society* in his pocket plus a speaking schedule that included a memorial to the Haymarket Martyrs, he was sent to Ellis Island to await deportation. Overnight, Emma organized the Free Speech League to contest the deportation, enlisted Clarence Darrow and Edgar Lee Masters as lawyers for the defense, and further organized a huge protest meeting at Cooper Union. Darrow and Masters managed to take the case all the way to the U.S. Supreme Court, declaring that the Exclusion Act was unconstitutional. And even if it *had* been constitutional, they argued,

Turner was only a philosophical anarchist and therefore not a threat to the government. The Court had ruled against them, and Turner had had to leave the country. Now, fourteen years later, Emma remembered only the glory of taking action.

The day after the Selective Service Act was passed, Emma and Sasha called a mass meeting in New York City of the No Conscription League, an organization they had founded a year earlier, and on May 18 eight thousand people packed the Harlem River Casino to hear the war denounced as an imperialist venture being fought on behalf of capitalists at the expense of workers. Remember, the speakers enjoined, at the end of every bayonet is a worker. Emma herself, it was said, spoke "as if possessed by divine fire."

Within the next few weeks, meeting after meeting of the League was called, with each one drawing thousands into the hall, while many more thousands remained standing outside; at one meeting there were an estimated five thousand inside and fifteen thousand outside; at another, two thousand inside and an estimated thirty-five thousand outside. Wisely, not one speaker urged young men to avoid draft registration. Later, when many of them were on trial, hundreds of undercover policemen could have testified that no one had ever mentioned draft registration at any of these meetings. But such fine distinctions were no longer to the point.

The June 1917 issue of *Mother Earth* carried the complete text of the No Conscription manifesto, and on the magazine's cover was a drawing of a coffin draped in black surrounded by the words "In Memoriam—American Democracy." On the 15th of that month, Emma and Sasha were arrested in the magazine's offices by a U.S. marshal accompanied by twelve city policemen. Emma changed into a royal purple dress, grabbed a small toilet case (always at the ready for police station confinements) and a copy of Joyce's *Portrait of the Artist as a Young Man* (a book was also always at the ready), and marched out, head held high. Next day she and Sasha were formally charged with conspiring to obstruct the draft. Meanwhile, their office, like the offices of every radical organization in the country, was being raided: letters, manuscripts, mailing lists, files, records, addresses, checkbooks were all confiscated and lost forever. But their bail (set at twenty-five thousand dollars each) was met by liberal supporters, and no sooner were they out on the street than they called a meeting.

The trial opened on July 2. Emma, who had just turned forty-eight, looked forward to mounting the soapbox of her dreams. "We have been able to do remarkable work," she and Sasha wrote to the faithful, "and if only we are not interrupted in our summing up it will be worth going to jail for the propaganda accomplished and that's the main thing, after all." Both Sasha and Emma conducted their own defense, and in the eyes of all—including the judge—each performance was a masterpiece of reasoned eloquence.

Emma spoke for an hour. She began by defending the right to conscientious objection in a democracy, especially when that objection was based on a hatred of the kind of organized bloodshed that war claimed necessary to secure "world justice." For the conscientious objector, Emma said, "The righteous passion for justice can never express itself in human slaughter." This conviction provided the force behind an objector's willingness to stand outside the law. It was a conviction that went so deep it superseded the natural desire, common to all, to stand shoulder to shoulder with one's fellow citizens in a time of national disaster.

She reminded her listeners that in times of crisis—like the one they were now facing—many good people are compelled to stand outside the law when that law goes against the higher dictates of a humanist conscience. Jesus, Socrates, Galileo—none had been within the law when they stood their ground on behalf of the truth as they saw it. By the same token, the Founding

Fathers of the American Revolution had defied the law in order to declare that law unjust; and certainly the great Civil War abolitionists had done the same, giving their life's blood to fight slavery when slavery was the law of the land. Each of those historic actors had challenged the law for the sake of speaking the truth when to so speak was to risk all. Turning directly to the jury, she added herself to this list: "Even if we were convicted and found guilty and the penalty was that we be placed against a wall and shot dead, I should nevertheless cry out with the great Luther, here I am and here I stand and I cannot do otherwise."

It was an irreducible human need that was at stake here: the need to speak one's mind freely, without fear of reprisal. Emma entreated the jurors to remember that whatever liberties they had today, they owed to the people who stood outside the law in the name of that need. These, she said, "were the Anarchists of their time," and they based their case on that claim to the right of free speech — the right upon which the entire history of democracy is based — as an essence of political liberty. The verdict in this case would tell the world whether here in America that right was to be honored or destroyed, whether it constituted "a living force . . . or a mere shadow of the past." The eyes of the whole country are upon you, she warned, "not because of sympathy for us or agreement with Anarchism. They are upon you because it must be decided sooner or later whether we are justified in telling people that we will give them democracy in Europe, when we have no democracy here."

The verdict was guilty. Nonetheless, being able to speak their piece in court left both Sasha and Emma feeling exhilarated. The August 1917 issue of *Mother Earth* — the magazine's last — carried an advertisement on the back cover for the "Trial and Speeches of Alexander Berkman and Emma Goldman: the complete account of the arrest, trial and conviction for their activities in the Anti-Conscription agitation, with their remarkable speeches in the U. S. District Court of New York, July

1917." And inside, Berkman and Goldman wrote their friends: "We are going to prison with light hearts. To us it is more satisfactory to stay behind bars than to remain MUZZLED in freedom." At this moment they felt they could take on anything—which was what they now had to do.

Unbelievably, between the time the trial ended and the time they were sentenced, Sasha was slapped with an extradition order from the State of California on a charge of murder. In one sense the charge came out of the blue, in another it was perfectly predictable. In an attempt to rev the country up for war, gung-ho patriots had come up with the idea of Preparedness Parades to be held in cities across the country, and in San Francisco one such parade had been set for July 22, 1916. Half an hour into the parade, a suitcase bomb had exploded, killing ten people and injuring forty. Within a short time, Tom Mooney and Warren Billings—members, respectively, of the radical Molders Union and the IWW—were charged with the crime. And now, a year later, simply because he had been in San Francisco at the time of the bombing, Sasha Berkman was being charged as well. There was never any hard evidence against him, but the State of California was demanding that he be brought west to stand trial alongside Mooney and Billings.

In New York everyone in the Goldman-Berkman circle was flabbergasted—everyone but Emma, who, out on bail, went right to work. Nothing could take her mind off her own impending imprisonment like organizing a protest. Within minutes she had the support of the United Hebrew Trades and the Amalgamated Clothing Workers Union, followed by the bookbinders, the furriers, and the typographers, and was organizing mass meetings at Cooper Union and the Brooklyn Labor Lyceum. Sasha was beloved on the Lower East Side, and the radical Yiddish press pulled out all the stops on his behalf. To the amazement of all, the extradition order was delayed (the charges were later dropped), and, ironically, Sasha's friends were relieved to see him troop off to jail in Atlanta, Georgia, where he was destined (as always) to do hard, hard time. As Sasha would be driven to denounce injustice whenever it came his way, repeatedly, throughout the next two years, all privileges—books, exercise, visitors—would be taken from him and solitary confinement inflicted again and again. Talk about living one's truth.

Sasha Berkman was an extraordinary bundle of extremes, exhibiting an aggressive compassion for comrades mixed equally with an aggressive contempt for those who served "the system." In the face of organized authority his anarchist temperament remained uninflected, and this throughout a lifetime of harassment by one government or another. After having spent fourteen years in jail for the attempted assassination of Henry Frick, the thought alone of prison made Sasha ill. Yet he prepared cheerfully to endure it once again, fortified by the depth of unconflicted ideological feeling that had ever anchored his politics and his personality. The key word, with Sasha, was *unconflicted*. In 1919, at the end of his prison term, when he was offered a hearing that might prevent his deportation, he refused grandly in the same tone of voice with which he had defended himself two years earlier in court. "The purpose of the present hearing," he lectured the government sternly, "is to determine my 'attitude of mind.' . . . It is purely an inquiry into my views and opinions. . . . I deny the right of anyone—individually or collectively—to set up an inquisition of thought. Thought is, or should be, free. My social views and political opinions are my personal concern. I owe no one responsibility for them. Responsibility begins only with the effects of thought expressed in action. Not before. Free thought, necessarily involving freedom of speech and press, I may tersely define thus: no opinion a law—no opinion a crime. For the government to attempt to control thought, to prescribe certain opinions or proscribe others, is the height of despotism. . . . This proposed hearing is an invasion of my conscience. I therefore refuse, most emphatically, to participate in it."

Emma, too, would ultimately have to refuse a hearing—for her, also, the terms were intolerable—but a pained love of America took her by surprise. The constant struggle for anarchism that she had waged there had become a part of her identity, a way of seeing herself that she associated with the country. It was in America, her biographer Alice Wexler tells us, that her "radical vision, broader and more encompassing than that of almost anyone else on the Left, had shocked, inspired, and educated thousands, both inside and outside the anarchist movement" and made hers "a powerful symbol of that 'spirit of revolt' which she defined as the essence of anarchism." Within that experience, she had come to love the America of the rebels, radicals, and dissenters—Emerson and Thoreau, Franklin and Whitman, Eugene Debs and Voltairine de Cleyr—and in the end she could hardly believe that the country refused to love her back. For all her denunciations of American tyranny, she wrote in her memoir, when the deportation order came she felt it as a knife in the heart. "Deportation for mere opinion's sake. Czarist Russia exiled people for revolutionary ideas—but not free America!" It was as though she cared more for the moral damage America was doing to itself than for the injustice being inflicted on her.

Sasha was astonished at how intensely Emma suffered at being forced to leave the United States, even though her final experience of the country—the last two years of imprisonment—had provided so concrete a reminder of the insult inflicted on the human spirit at the hands of the state that, clearly, there wasn't a government in the world with which she could ever make her peace.

Emma Goldman entered the Missouri State Penitentiary in Jefferson City on February 6, 1918, prepared to become a model prisoner—calm, kindly, resourceful, a motherly arbiter who would work unceasingly to achieve greater sympathy between the prisoners and the prison authorities—not because she feared those authorities but because she held prison life in awe. Life "inside" was one of those realities that threw an anarchist's obsession with the irreducible needs of humanity into relief as nothing else could. Jail was human deprivation on a scale that was existential in its nature: it had to be felt in the flesh to be understood. "Daily," Sasha Berkman had written in his prison memoirs, "I behold the machinery at work, grinding and pulverizing, brutalizing the officers, dehumanizing the inmates . . . [a life] agonizing and merciless within the walls." The starkness of *this* reality far outstripped that of any other.

In 1918, in the Missouri penitentiary for women, prisoners survived under conditions of permanent low-grade sadism. Routinely, and for the most arbitrary of reasons, they were deprived of food or exercise, went untreated when ill, were forced into illegal and demeaning labor, were beaten when deemed disobedient, and were thrown into solitary confinement at the drop of a retort. Outstripping all of this in its power to demoralize was the daily anxiety about not completing "the task"— the term given in jail to the allotted amount of work a prisoner was commanded to perform daily—which in the Missouri penitentiary meant sewing clothes at a rate of production and under conditions that resembled life in a concentration camp. Each prisoner, without exception or allowance, had to produce daily 45 to 121 jackets, 9 to 18 dozen sets of suspenders, or an equal number of overalls or coats, regardless of whether she were sick or crazed or lacked the requisite skill or strength to sit at the machine. If she didn't complete the quota she would lose whatever privileges she had coming—including food or visitors or open-air exercise—and she would be punished. Punishments ranged from being flogged to being locked up and fed bread and water to being thrown into solitary confinement (otherwise known as "the hole").

The punishments themselves were bad enough, but the worst of it was that they reduced a prisoner's hope of getting time off for good behavior, which was tantamount to extending her sentence. This constant threat of having to do what was felt to be extra time induced a kind of mass dread that was physically as well as mentally draining. The women bartered for everything—for clothing, cigarettes, a book or a newspaper— but for nothing as desperately as a way to fulfill the daily quota if for one reason or another they felt unable to do it themselves. Nothing, not the boredom, not the regimentation, not the punishments, produced as much despair as walking into "the shop" where the threat of doing additional time hung palpably in the air.

Emma's quota was thirty-six jackets a day, and while the work was exhausting (often frighteningly so), she never failed to make it. This, along with her impeccable behavior, gave her a peculiar status. Many of the guards felt free to despise her as a political prisoner, but as the dignified, unassuming persona she had now adopted she was accorded the unusual respect of the prisoners, and thus the warden sought to exploit her usefulness by offering her the stewardship of the shop, a privileged position she adamantly refused to take. She could not, she explained, be a boss over anyone. The other inmates—all of whom were in prison on criminal charges of one sort or another, up to and including murder—barely understood who she was or what she was in for. Political prisoner? what the hell did that mean? But no matter: they understood her refusal to lord it over them. No sooner did the word spread that she'd refused the stewardship than, with exponential speed, she gained their affection and, more important, their trust.

Emma Goldman was not often experienced as a friend to women—most of the women she knew found her patronizing or dismissive—but in prison all questions of ego dropped away, and all fears of intimacy were rendered magnificently irrelevant. What remained was a sense of identification with the other inmates that brought her not only into close human relationships, but into visceral contact with her own politics. Emma never thought of the women with whom she served time as criminals. She saw each one as a person so damaged by society that apology rather than punishment was what was due her. "Poor wretches," she wrote to a friend, driven by "the world of poverty and drabness" into which they'd been born to do whatever it was they had done (who but Emma would have applied the word *drabness* to explain the cause of the behavior of a thief, a prostitute, a drug addict?). There was nothing that a prisoner could tell Emma that she would find off-putting. Inevitably, she supplied the empathic understanding a woman needed not to feel abstract to herself. The relief the women experienced at feeling free to confide in her was enough to make of Emma a prized person; even so, they were amazed by the all-in-allness of her comradeship. Not only did she share the packages of food, clothing, and books that came regularly to her; she intervened time and again for them when they were mistreated; helped fill their quotas when they were sick; organized for the installation of showers, sanitized cells, decent food; and above all militated constantly for a reduction in all the little humiliations that made a prisoner feel less than human. Take the incident of the picnic.

The warden, Emma felt, was quite a decent fellow. Following her lead, he decided, as a measure of enlightened reform, to allow the inmates a picnic in a nearby local park every other Saturday, with music to be supplied by an orchestra composed of the prisoners themselves. It was the hope of the prison authorities that a "new morale" would emerge from this experiment in extended privilege. The women were beside themselves with joy, as was Emma herself. When they got to the park, however, it turned out that their activity was to be restricted to a section of the park no bigger than the prison yard, and heavily armed guards were to walk ahead of and behind them at all times; also, they could not approach the orchestra directly as it, too, was surrounded by armed guards. The event, notwithstanding the fresh air, was a disaster: they might just as well have never left the jail.

The warden was bewildered by the dismal failure of his effort at liberal largesse, and Emma worked hard to make him see what had gone wrong. The women's feeling, she told him, "that at least once in two weeks they are [to be] given a chance to eliminate the prison from their consciousness" had been betrayed. How could it be otherwise with the guards acting as though they weren't, in the slightest, to be trusted? That was a posture bound to come a cropper. "Don't you see?" she explained patiently. "It's not the park that will prove an influence for good. It will be your trust in [them]." Give the prisoners the sense of release that comes with being even minimally trusted and you will "create a new morale among [them]." Otherwise, these paltry efforts are for naught. Remarkably, the warden took her point, and the next time out, the prisoners had the run of the park with the guards pacing in the background.

Emma spent her fiftieth birthday in prison. On that day, her intimates among the prisoners insisted on completing her task for her.

No sooner was she released from prison, on September 27, 1919, than she, along with Sasha, was re-arrested and brought to court by J. Edgar Hoover, newly appointed head of the General Intelligence Division of the Bureau of Investigation (still operating within the Justice Department), who persuaded the government to begin deportation proceedings. A mass of stunned and sorrowing friends threw a farewell party—at which Sasha, upon learning that Henry Frick had just died, remarked drily, "Deported by God"—and on December 21 they, along with 247 other foreign-born radicals, were placed aboard the *Buford*, a barely seaworthy relic of the Spanish-American

War that convinced its passengers that the U.S. government cared not whether they lived or died. Twenty-eight days later, the leaky ship docked at a Finnish port, whereupon the deportees were transferred to a train that took them to the Russian border. Once on Soviet soil they were met by a government committee, which greeted them warmly and welcomed them to the People's State.

Grief stricken as she was (and she was) at having been forced out of the United States, Emma was intensely excited at the thought of joining the Russian Revolution. "Soviet Russia!" she rhapsodized in her memoir, recalling the sentiment with which, at the beginning of 1920, she approached her return to the now transformed land of her birth. "Sacred ground, magic people, destined to redeem mankind. I have come to serve you, *matushka*. Take me to your bosom, let me pour myself into you, mingle my blood with yours, find my place in your heroic struggle, and give to the uttermost to your needs."

It is impossible to overestimate what the Russian Revolution meant to people like Emma Goldman. On the night of March 15, 1917—the day the tsar abdicated—fifteen thousand people filled New York's Madison Square Garden; up in Harlem (then also a neighborhood of immigrant Jews) another huge rally was taking place; downtown on the Lower East Side thousands gathered in Seward Park to read the bulletins of the Yiddish dailies which were being posted hourly. In the cafés, in the synagogues, on street corners, the immigrant world was erupting in a round-the-clock party that was reported on with near disbelief by the mainstream press. Men in the street could not stop smiling and clapping one another on the back, women laughed, cried, and embraced. It was as though a century of revolutionary hope were being channeled through these people. Then, on November 8, the Bolsheviks seized power—and everyone went crazy with pro-Soviet joy. As Abe Cahan, the editor of the social democratic *Forward* (and ultimately a violent enemy of the Soviet Union), wrote that week, "Who can help rejoicing in their triumph? Who can help going into ecstasy over the Socialist spirit with which they have enthroned the country, which they now rule?"

Immigrant New Yorkers were hardly alone in their delirium over the Russian Revolution. All over the world, liberals and radicals—workers, teachers, students; housewives, artists, intellectuals—were throwing their hats in the air and preparing to tell their children and grandchildren where they were when they heard that the tsar had been deposed. Goldman herself, although an enemy of organized Marxism, wrote ecstatically about the historic promise that the Bolshevik takeover represented. Emma was not ignorant of how things stood between Russian anarchists and the Bolsheviks, but at that moment a wave of revolutionary sentiment was washing all her analytic hard-headedness out to sea.

The history of anarchism in Russia—encompassing, much like that of anarchism elsewhere, communists, individualists, and labor unionists (syndicalists)—had, inevitably, been one of bitter conflict. Marxists and anarchists alike despised bourgeois reform as much as they had loathed the tsarist regime, but that did not prevent them from feeling a visceral hatred for one another. Immediately after the Revolution started, they worked together in a number of places and on many projects, but when the anarchists saw that the Bolsheviks wanted party power, not worker control, they grew violently critical of the regime. The Bolsheviks, in turn, unable to tolerate any degree of independent thought, much less action, instantly declared the anarchists enemies of the state, and within a year were making war on them. In April 1918 the Bolshevik government raided every anarchist center in Moscow, killing many and jailing more than five hundred, almost all of whom were still in prison when the *Buford* docked in Finland.

Nonetheless, a headiness of revolutionary enthusiasm made

both Emma and Sasha put aside, for the moment, the thought that the Soviet Union might see them as potential enemies. They arrived in Saint Petersburg (now called Petrograd) more than ready to have bourgeois American rejection undone by a revolutionary Russian welcome—only to leave the country two years later permanently scarred by what they had lived through under the Bolsheviks. In her 1923 memoir *My Disillusionment in Russia*—a book that ultimately alienated the left as well as the right—Emma recapitulates the entire experience. To read the book is to relive it with her.

To begin with, she rehearses her love of and belief in the Russian people, her bottomless admiration for their resilience, and her emotional understanding of why they, of all oppressed peoples, had been able to overthrow their aristocratic rulers. The orthodox Marxist view that a revolution could not take place in any but an industrially advanced country had failed to take something more vital than industrial development into consideration: a hunger for liberty nurtured by decades of revolutionary agitation coupled with a lack of political sophistication on the part of the peasantry. This had proved crucial.

Unacquainted with "the subtleties of politics, of parliamentary trickery, and legal makeshifts," Russians shared a "primitive sense of justice and right [that] was strong and vital, without the disintegrating finesse of pseudo-civilization." Thus, mass response to the agitating acts of early 1917 had ripened "at so fast a pace that within a few months the people were ready for such ultra-revolutionary slogans as 'All power to the Soviets' and 'The land to the peasants, the factories to the workers,'" and in June and July of that historic year these slogans were "enthusiastically and actively taken up in the form of direct action by the bulk of the industrial and agrarian population of more than 150 millions." The peasants began to expropriate the land while the workers took possession of the factories without paying attention to the fact that according to Marx they were not developed enough to make a revolution.

Of course, she goes on, to make the Revolution work — that is, to achieve economic and social reconstruction — the co-operative genius of the entire people was required; and, indeed, "This spirit of mutual purpose and solidarity swept Russia with a mighty wave in the first days of the October/November Revolution. Inherent in that enthusiasm were forces that could have moved mountains if intelligently guided by exclusive consideration for the well-being of the whole people. The medium for such effective guidance was on hand: the labor organizations and the cooperatives with which Russia was covered as with a network of bridges combining the city with the country; the Soviets which sprang into being, responsive to the needs of the Russian people; and, finally, the intelligentsia whose traditions for a century expressed heroic devotion to the cause of Russia's emancipation." But it soon transpired that the hopes such infrastructure promised were not to be realized.

And here begins Emma's long, hard, unyielding accusation against the party of Lenin for placing a calculated stranglehold on the honest spirit of revolution that had brought down the most primitive monarchy in the world. True enough, a fantastic chaos had overtaken Russia no sooner was the tsar gone. The revolutionary government — composed of ideologues who had absolutely no experience in running anything, much less a government — was beleaguered first by European war, then by civil war and foreign intervention, and finally by an economy that was unraveling hourly, as private industry and trade had been abolished and the newly constructed state did not know how to perform its functions. Domestic disorganization threatened total breakdown.

At the same time, ironically, because the Bolshevik government didn't really know what to do about "culture" yet —

it would remain for Stalin to figure that one out—the 1920s were a time of unparalleled freedom in the arts. Music, literature, film, the plastic arts—through them a brilliant mixture of revolutionary excitement and modernist exhilaration was pouring out of Russia in those years. Nonetheless, what Emma and Sasha began quickly to see (and soon it was all they saw) was that for the Communist Party, life had become primarily a matter of concentrating power in its own hands. The solid block of authoritarianism that was met with everywhere in early 1920 shocked and frightened first Emma, then Sasha.

Wherever one turned, the omnipresent political machine was in evidence. In the unions, in the cooperatives, in the local soviets: not a single place of work was without the superfluous, even menacing presence of a party representative, saturating the atmosphere with a sense of suspicion and surveillance that induced anxiety and inhibition. No one felt free to exercise initiative, speak his or her mind openly, argue, suggest, or implement. Besides, no matter what decisions might be taken locally, all activity either went forward or stood still depending on permission granted from party headquarters. There might be fuel in Petrograd where people were freezing, farming materials in the fields where people longed to plant, even food in the stores where people were going hungry, but nothing was distributed or acted upon until orders were received from Moscow—that is, from Communist Party bureaucrats—often men without experience or judgment or even goodwill who were calling the shots from the Kremlin.

Equally upsetting was the constant sight of gross inequality, with party privileges regularly being granted within full view of the ordinary citizen. There were thirty-three categories of pay with different food rations—this under communism!—for each class of worker, most of whom could not afford to buy butter at two thousand rubles a pound, or sugar at three thousand, or meat at one thousand. Yet everyone could see excellent foodstuffs being delivered to party officials while workers stood for hours in the cold, waiting for "frozen potatoes, wormy cereal, decayed fish." This situation, in those early days, could often induce a vocal anger that in the years ahead would be remembered as refreshing. Once, in a communal kitchen, Emma saw a peasant girl come in and ask for vinegar, at that time a luxury. She was the servant of Grigory Zinoviev, one of Lenin's major confidants and a member of the Central Committee. When the girl referred to Zinoviev as her master, a storm of indignation broke loose. "Master!" someone cried. "Is that what we made the Revolution for, or was it to do away with masters?" A few years later Emma recalled the moment fondly. Who in Russia today, she then thought, would dare to criticize a party official so openly?

Even more dismaying was the conflict between the workers and the intelligentsia, an antagonism the party fed by pushing a line about education and culture being bourgeois prejudices that the Russian people could easily do without. Those who made art and demonstrated intellect, the government all but announced, were unnecessary to the Revolution. In fact, they were probably its enemies.

It had always been Sasha and Emma's intention to meet with Lenin in the hope of intervening on behalf of their beleaguered comrades, but when, after many months in the country, the two at last gained an interview with him they were received with a courtesy that quickly wore thin, revealing the low value set upon their presence in the country. Sasha asked about all the anarchists in jail, and Lenin replied irritably that there are no anarchists in jail, only criminals. Emma asked about the lack of freedom of speech, and Lenin told her coldly that freedom of speech was a bourgeois luxury; the Revolution had more important things on its mind. When they reported Peter Kropotkin's argument that only the restoration of independent trade unions, soviets, and peasant cooperatives could save the revolution, Lenin told them to go find some useful work to do and stop worrying about things they didn't understand. At last they were ushered out of the office, never again to lay eyes on the great Bolshevik leader.

Although they were subsisting on a government stipend— this much recognition they were accorded as Friends of the Revolution—they wandered about for months, from Petrograd to Moscow, back to Petrograd, back out into the country— restless, lonely, and confused, unable to find useful work, much less stability and purposefulness, or even (worse yet) a single soul with whom to commiserate. There were other American leftists in Russia at the time—John Reed and Bill Haywood, for instance—but these were true believers who quickly grew irritated if not downright angry with Emma and Sasha's critical stance. In Moscow, Haywood came up for a cup of Emma's famous coffee ("black as night, sweet as love, strong as revolutionary zeal"), but soon ended up quarreling with her. In time Haywood would denounce both Goldman and Berkman as critics who blamed the Soviet Union because the Bolsheviks had not given them the cushy positions they'd expected to receive.

The final blow comes when Emma decides to get in touch with Maxim Gorki. "He would understand the struggle going on within me," she thinks, knocking on the apartment door of the famous writer, whom she remembers as an early critic of the Bolsheviks. Now, however, she finds him weary and ill, with a bad cough, sounding like an apologist. It is obvious, though, even from her own account, that whatever his own misgivings about his country's faltering revolution, Gorki, too, is drawn up short by her unsympathetic complaints, and does not wish to make common cause with her. When she leads with "the problem of persecution and terror—were all the horrors inevitable, or was there some fault in Bolshevism itself?" Gorki replies drily that no doubt the Bolsheviks were making mistakes, but as far as he could see, "they were doing the best they knew how, nothing more could be expected."

Having hit a wall on politics, she then tries to make connection through literature, and this nails the lid on the coffin of their exchange. In 1914 Goldman had published a collection of essays on the social significance of contemporary European drama: Ibsen, Shaw, Strindberg. The book sank like a stone — Margaret Anderson described the essays as deeply marred by the endless "intrusion of dogma and platitude into the discussion, the wearying insistence upon 'the moral' of each play, and the uncritical acquiescence in the veracity of each dramatic picture of life." Yet Goldman considered herself an expert on the subject. "By way of introduction," she writes, "I had shown Gorki an announcement card of the dramatic course I had given in America. John Galsworthy was among the playwrights I had discussed then." This did not sit at all well with Gorki. He "expressed surprise that I considered Galsworthy an artist. In his opinion Galsworthy could not be compared with Bernard Shaw. I had to differ. I did not underestimate Shaw, but considered Galsworthy the greater artist. I detected irritation in Gorki, and as his hacking cough continued, I broke off the discussion."

All in all, she comes away from her meeting with the Great Writer utterly dejected. The interview had given her nothing but an increased sense of isolation. One can just imagine how Gorki felt, trapped between Goldman's hard-edged negativism coupled with her unsophisticated literary criticism and his own increasingly ill-making anxieties.

Life steadily became a bad dream, and the worst of it was that the source of the dream did not lie wholly with external circumstances. "What made Russia so overwhelming an experience for [Emma]," writes Alice Wexler, "was its challenge to her deepest sense of personal identity . . . when she found that she had no place in an actual revolution." In his own way,

Sasha was coming to terms with much the same insight. He was seeing, with a clarity not to be denied, that anarchism as they knew it prepared one for nothing on the ground. What, after all, did an anarchist do the day after the revolution? Who knew how to organize anything—take responsibility, delegate power, end the childish quarreling endemic to anarchist meetings? Side by side, Emma and Sasha were staring into separate but similar voids. So they wandered on, trapped, as in a dream, in a numbing stasis, until the dream began to morph into nightmare.

Then came Kronstadt—and suddenly stasis was moot.

On March 1, 1921, an uprising took place, led by the sailors in the Kronstadt fortress, home of the Soviet Baltic fleet in the Gulf of Finland. Out of it came a petition to the government of thirteen demands, among them freedom of speech, the right to free elections in their own soviet, the right of assembly, and the liberation of all political prisoners. The fortress was thirty-five miles from Petrograd. Fearing (rightly) that the protest would spread to the city, the Bolshevik government decided on suppression rather than negotiation. Exactly one week after the uprising, the Red Army, under Leon Trotsky's command, opened fire on the fortress. Thousands were killed, and Kronstadt went down in history as the first public demonstration of the Terror that would engulf the Soviet Union for the next seventy years.

When it was over, Emma wrote years later, she was haunted by the stillness that had fallen on Petrograd—this "city drenched in blood"—and knew for certain that the revolution she had believed in all her life was now a caricature "come to jeer and mock me." This deformity created a pain, she said, that ate "more into one's vitals than the existence of reaction in other lands."

Immediately after Kronstadt, Emma and Sasha severed all connection with the government and decided to leave the country. Between that moment and the moment they actually got out, in December, they came close to destitution. "Without their government rations and privileges," the writer Alix Kates Shulman recounts, they were forced to move into a small, seedy apartment in Moscow, where "they had to collect and chop their own firewood, lugging it miles through the snow and up three flights of stairs on their feeble backs. They had to fetch water twice a day from a long distance. They had to cook and wash everything themselves, like the poorest workers." But their pain and exhaustion, Emma later said, "were as nothing to our inner liberation."

Emma and Sasha left the Soviet Union twenty-three months after they had arrived. One more year and, in all probability, they would have ended up in a labor camp in Siberia.

Now they were truly in exile, stateless in every sense of the word. In the United States, every agency that had a stake in their never again setting foot in America—Immigration, Justice, the military—seemed to become unhinged upon learning of Emma and Sasha's departure from Russia. J. Edgar Hoover himself alerted every intelligence agency in Europe to the danger of giving these world-famous terrorists asylum and had their photographs sent to officials at every border and port of entry throughout the West.

Years later, in the thirties, Goldman wrote a piece called "The Tragedy of the Political Exiles" in which she described the lot of political refugees from 1918 on. Before the war, she said, all radicals could easily come and go. "In those days who cared about passports or visas? Who worried about one particular spot on earth? The whole world was one's country. One place was as good as another where one could continue one's work for the liberation of one's autocratic native land. Not in their wildest dream did it occur to these revolutionaries that the time might come when the world would be turned into a huge penitentiary. . . . The war for democracy and the advent of the left and right dictatorships destroyed whatever freedom of movement political refugees formerly enjoyed. Tens of thousands of men, women, and children have been turned into modern Ahasueruses [Wandering Jews], forced to roam the earth, admitted nowhere, their lives made a veritable hell."

Emma and Sasha came out of Russia into Riga, where they were immediately informed by the authorities that they were unwelcome in Latvia: stay a few days or weeks, then you must push on. Next came Stockholm, where they were told the same; this time, a month's visa was extended them. Then Berlin, where they met with more of the same. They were on an international blacklist that was turning their lives into a bureaucratic nightmare. In each capital, the authorities were waiting to delay, expel, or imprison them. Their days were often spent at consulate desks where clerks half their age felt free to ignore or sneer or ridicule. "Come back tomorrow at three," one would say. "Wednesday at ten," instructed another. "A week from now at six," ordered a third.

Stockholm offered a breather. Here both Sasha and Emma began to write the articles on the Russian experience upon which their mutual attention was concentrated. Emma especially was possessed of so urgent a sense of mission—the world must *know*—that she felt justified in taking extreme measures. When the New York *World* offered her a contract for a series of pieces on Bolshevik Russia she accepted, though Sasha demurred, quarreling over the rightness of publishing in the bourgeois press, whereupon—she tells the readers of her memoir—she announced, "I must cry out against the gigantic deception posing as truth and justice!"

There are hundreds of sentences throughout her memoir that Emma tells us she either spoke or thought which sound hardly credible—after all, who talks like that? But the self-heroizing rhetoric is an important part of what held her together; it can well be believed that the purple prose inside her head, as well as on the page, acted often to ennoble the ridiculous—thereby permitting "the work" to go on. Here's a great example:

In Stockholm, in the midst of the ongoing tumult over the threat of imminent expulsion, with the whole world denying her a place to live, and the clock ticking on their Swedish visa, Emma manages to fall in love with a thirty-year-old Swede (she's now fifty-two), who wants only to learn about "life" and "anarchy" at Emma's knee—and is willing to share her bed in order to do so. For three months (Sweden extends the visa) the two carry on an affair. Then, of course, it is over. Which means that Emma must suffer, which also means that she can't get down to work on the prospective book on Russia. There follow weeks of mooning about—the end of the affair is always an occasion for ceremonial distress—but finally she shakes it off, and is now working around the clock. After a stormy, rain-soaked night of steady writing, the dawn arrives: "The storm outside had stopped. The air was still, the sun slowly rising and spreading its red and gold over the sky in a greeting of the new day. I wept, conscious of the eternal rebirth in nature, in the dreams of man, in his quest for freedom and beauty, in the struggle of humanity to greater heights. I felt the re-birth of my own life, to blend once more with the universal of which I was but an infinitesimal part." Can't beat that for getting over the failed sex blues.

In Berlin, with Sasha at her side, reading and editing her every word—he must often have felt bitter over the fact that while the material was shared, it was always *she* who had the burning energy to make first use of it—she did indeed write the book that revealed "the colossal fraud wrapped in the Red mantle of October." But this was one piece of work destined to give no satisfaction. When it was finally published (in 1923) by Doubleday in America, its title had been changed from *My Two Years in Russia* to *My Disillusionment in Russia*, and the second half of the book—the analysis, which she considered the most vital part—had been omitted. Not only did this publication outrage Emma because of the butchery of her work (as it would any writer), it brought down on her a storm of left-wing abuse from which there would be no recovery. This was a moment—it would prove a very long one—when nearly the entire left was in love with the Russian Revolution, and apostasy received no understanding, much less forgiveness.

In the summer of 1924 a grand dinner was given for her in London, where most of the intelligentsia had not yet read the book. Two hundred and fifty people—among them Rebecca West, Havelock Ellis, Edward Carpenter, H. G. Wells, the writer and political activist Israel Zangwill, Bertrand Russell—had come out on a stormy night to hear the great Emma Goldman speak. The evening was a disaster. Later, Bertrand Russell wrote, "When she rose to speak, she was welcomed enthusiastically; but when she sat down, there was dead silence. This was because almost the whole speech was against the Bolsheviks." For the liberal left *this* was betrayal. Even if everything she said were true (which it simply couldn't be), this was not the right time to supply ammunition to the enemies of the fledgling Revolution. One by one, everyone at the dinner except the stalwart Rebecca West rose and left. Emma was stupefied. Not the right time to speak? The time to speak is the moment one learns the truth. That is the right time. That is *always* the right time.

Now she found herself triply cast out: alienated from an exhausted postwar world in which political activism held no allure; harassed by government authorities who continued to see her as a threat to the state; separated from a weakened European and American left which shrank, repelled, from her denunciation of the Bolsheviks.

Even she could see that her position was bizarre. From London she wrote to Sasha, "My situation is really a desperate one. The Tories have taken a stand against the communists, in France they are being hounded, the Pope comes out against them. And here am I doing the same. It is no wonder everybody refuses to join me. It really means working hand in glove with the reactionaries. On the other hand, I know I must go ahead and that our position is of a different nature." The evils of industrial capitalism retreated visibly to a back burner of political concern. The "truth about Russia" had now become an overriding passion. The world, she obsessed, *must* speak out against the Soviets' betrayal of the Revolution.

But it wasn't really Bolshevism Emma was objecting to, it was Marxism itself. The important thing to realize, she said and kept on saying, was that *any* Marxian revolution was bound to end in a dictatorship. The key lay in the Marxists' conviction that the ends justify the means. "There is no greater fallacy," she wrote, "than the belief that aims and purposes are one thing, while methods and tactics another. The means used to prepare the future become its cornerstone."

Such an analysis was devastating to the socialist movement as a whole; it was the kind of judgment that drained it of all hope of improvement from within. Countless leftists were devoted to the creation of a genuine socialist democracy, imagining that the severe measures being taken in the Soviet Union were temporary. Of necessity, these people could see themselves as nothing but revolutionary Marxists. Yet here was Emma Goldman telling them that their dreams were delusional, that Marxism itself was a flawed theory which, once put into practice, could end in nothing but tyranny. No one on the left in 1924 could swallow such an indictment. One by one, they fell away from her.

The alienation of so many who for so long had been warmhearted comrades was painful indeed; but Emma shrugged — she was used to being "excommunicated," she said — and wore her anti-Bolshevism like a badge of honor. In a sense that badge put iron in her soul. Adrift in exile, deprived of a platform in the daily life of a single culture, she made her steady denunciation of the Soviet Union an anchor: a fixed point that helped her understand who she was and where she was. For the rest of her days, whenever she was at a loss for an issue, she would reorient herself by focusing on the evils of the Soviet state.

Emma Goldman has often (and rightly) been praised as a courageous early critic of Soviet dictatorship, but in the view of many (including this biographer) her analysis of Russia in 1920 and 1921 was so overwhelmingly negative—a black-and-white depiction of what was still only a revolution in trouble, not yet a fully formed totalitarian state—that, as Alice Wexler puts it, it ultimately helped "lay the foundations of a caricature of Russian history that served interests profoundly hostile to her own." It also allowed her to avoid taking a hard look at her own movement, whose theoretical and practical limitations the Russian Revolution had brought to glaring light. Anarchism in 1920 was, in Emma's own words, in "a sort of trance," sadly in need of intellectual revitalization. But neither she nor Sasha was prepared to undertake such a project; instead, they contented themselves with repeating the catechism of general anarchist principles and denouncing the Bolshevik anti-Christ. In the end, Emma suffered more than she profited from her obsessive anticommunism. It dissipated her energies and in a strange way left her mind and spirit more adrift than ever.

Emma remained in England throughout 1924, trying to make the British respond to her sense of urgency, meeting at every turn with an intolerable coldness of both climate and culture. A horrifying sense of the fragmentation of the anarchist world began to overtake her; suddenly she realized that not only was she alone, she was abandoned. For the moment, an uncharacteristic bitterness laid her low. "Often I think," she wrote to a comrade, "that we revolutionists are like the capitalist system, we drain men and women of the best that is in them and then stand quietly by to see them end their days in destitution and loneliness." In other words, Why am I—I who have given so much to the movement—not being rescued?

Emma's sense of entitlement was no greater than that of any other public person who is celebrated every day for decades as the center of a world, and considering that grandiosity is the obverse of self-pity, she wasn't acting too badly; but the black depression that she fell into in England included the very real prospect of financial as well as spiritual destitution. For the first time in years she had to think about how to stay alive: "Not till my deportation had I ever given a thought to this question; I had felt that as long as I could use my voice and pen I could easily earn my living." Anarchism, however, had lost its romantic cachet, and the communists were breaking up her meetings. So now she was using her pen and her voice—writing and lecturing—but bringing in next to nothing. This new anxiety over money was complicated by a growing fear of never again being able to move freely about the world. "Our people simply do not realize," she wrote a friend, "what it means to be cast out from the whole world, the feeling of being absolutely adrift, it is the worst I have ever experienced, and I have known some hardships in my time."

It was here in London, at this time, that she realized she must have a passport—and she set out to do what she could have done years ago in New York but had sworn never to do: gain citizenship through marriage. Sasha wouldn't dream of seeking citizenship anywhere; he had settled down to spend the rest of his life in the south of France, perched precariously on one visa extension after another. For Emma, the prospect of such confinement was stifling. Citizenship was necessary, it mattered neither where nor through whom. The word went out, and in 1925 a sixty-five-year-old anarchist and Welsh miner, James Colton, went through the ceremony with her. Presto, Emma Goldman was a British citizen. She experienced this act as one of real capitulation, and it aged her. However, she was now free to come and go as she pleased—everywhere except to the United States—and it pleased her to go. England—cold cold cold—remained her least favorite country.

A circle of anarchists in exile had formed in the south of France, where many old comrades lived within an hour or two of one another (Sasha Berkman and Emmy Eckstein, the last of his many longtime companions, were settled in Nice). Friends of the anarchists like Margaret Anderson, the English journalist Frank Harris, and the American heiress Peggy Guggenheim and her husband, Lawrence Vail, were also living on that coast, and it was here with these like-minded people that Emma began to recover a sense of her own value. When in 1926 a cottage called Bon Esprit was found in the fishing village of Saint-Tropez, she let the super-rich Guggenheim buy it for her.

Encouraged to write her long-promised memoir, she settled into the cottage and prepared to do just that. But how was she to live? Where was the money to come from that would allow her to work undisturbed for a couple of years? Not to worry, these friends reassured her. People all over the world will support this project. Like an exiled queen indulging the loyal subjects who are now her intermediaries with the world at large, Emma allowed her friends to start fund raising. In no time, a committee was formed, with its headquarters in New York, and the Emma Goldman Memoirs Fund became a going concern. Remember, Emma announced grandly, no money would be accepted that had any strings attached, *and* she must pass on every letter that went out of that office.

But the money did not flow in, certainly not as it would have done twenty years earlier, before the war, when both Emma Goldman and anarchism were at the height of their influence. Now the lack of response from so many donors they had absolutely counted on left the fund raisers startled indeed. No one was prepared to take in the implications of such an outcome, least of all Emma. She decided that she would simply

help the Fund along herself. It was now that she persuaded
Leon Malmed—the delicatessen owner with whom she would
soon have an affair—to sponsor her on a tour of Canada.

Later she realized that by the time her boat had sailed from
Europe she was already in the grip of old fantasies, wild hopes
surging up as once again she hit the road for love and anarchism. If she had taken a youth-renewing potion, she could
not have been more glowingly energetic than she was on her
arrival in Canada. But the tour itself was a jolting disappointment—the crowds were gone, the money dribbled in—and the
love affair an absurdity. Both were signaling a future in which
everything would become a pale imitation of her former life.
However, Emma saw no handwriting on the wall. When the
tour and the affair fell to pieces, instead of growing thoughtful
she grew depressed and angry.

Back once more at Bon Esprit, the cottage, the garden,
the ocean breeze were a welcome respite from the turmoil of
Canada; but that is all the place would ever be to her—a respite—as it was for most of her guests-in-exile. There is a photo
of Emma and her friends taken sometime around 1928 having
lunch on the terrace of Bon Esprit, surrounded by the sheer
gorgeousness of the place—the light, the flowers, the hint of
the distant sea—and they are all looking stunned. What are we
doing here? their faces seem to say. This is all so unreal. We be-
long in the city, any city.

Emma wanted Sasha to come live with her while she wrote
her memoir. Now, as always, she needed him by her side during
this important undertaking. Sasha, however, living in Nice with
Emmy, could not readily oblige. The situation was, as it would
be for the rest of their lives, a thorn in everyone's side.

Sasha Berkman had not been Emma's lover since their
earliest youth together, but he was *the* vital connection in her
life. It was with him and him alone that she felt completely
herself: honest, rational, intellectually accountable (he was the

only person, throughout the years, who could criticize her with impunity). She craved his presence always. There was hardly a moment when she was not overflowing with the affection due him as the most courageous anarchist she would ever know, the greatest and most steadfast of comrades, the key witness to her life. And Sasha felt the same about her. Their correspondence reveals an exchange between equals of a rare and admirable sort.

But the years in prison had left Sasha emotionally disfigured, and afterward he could fall in love only with one inexperienced young woman after another, all of them adoring and uncritical. It was what he needed to survive. Now, in the last part of his life, he was living with a woman twenty years his junior, this one nervous, volatile, insecure, and slavishly devoted. One would have thought that for Sasha's sake, Emma and Emmy might have made common cause. But no, they were at loggerheads from the get-go, each jealous of Sasha's attentions, each accumulating grievances against the other, each competing for more time with the man she hungered to call her own. Emma's behavior was by far the worse. She acted like a mother in competition with a daughter-in-law, and her style of attack was maddening. My dear Emmy, she might write after an argument, it goes without saying that I love you as I would anyone who is as good to Sasha as you are, but when you do what you did the other night, Emmy dear, you must see that it only serves to produce distress all around. And then—all patronizing patience—she would analyze the event entirely in terms of Emmy's childish and destructive behavior. Meanwhile, back in Nice, Emmy would be tearing her hair about Emma's bad behavior "the other night," and if Sasha had had any hair (he was bald) he would have been clutching his, too.

Now in 1929 Emma chided Sasha for refusing to be separated from Emmy long enough to help her with the book and, in desperation, suggested that they both come to Bon Esprit for the duration. Here Sasha drew the line. He couldn't do that, he said, because of her "squelching effect" on other women, particularly the women in his life. "You are too strong for them," he told her, rather generously, "and they feel it, consciously or unconsciously, but every one of them has always felt it, without a single exception."

This really got to her, and she let loose, reminding him of all the grief he and other men in the movement had caused her over her affairs with younger men. This was something she'd been wanting to write about for a long time, the double standard by which the anarchists lived, *just like everyone else:* "It is nonsense to say that the attitude toward men and women in their love for younger people is the same. . . . Hundreds and hundreds of men marry women much younger than themselves; they have circles of friends, they are accepted by the world. This does not happen to women, not one in a million has a love affair for any length of time with a man younger than herself. If she has, she is the butt of her dearest friends and gradually becomes that in her own eyes. . . . Everybody objects, resents, in fact dislikes a woman who lives with a younger man; they think her a goddamned fool; no doubt she is that, but it is not the business or concern of friends to make her look and feel like a fool."

The Emmy-Sasha-Emma imbroglio remained at a hopeless stalemate, with Emma constantly announcing that she was being mistreated. The relationship itself rankled, reminding her always of the bewildering loneliness that now, in increasing age, seemed like an unearned punishment rather than the inevitable consequence of a lifetime of choices she had felt compelled to make. Sasha, caught between the two exactly like a son between a mother and a wife, was the one most often to get it in the neck, especially when a deed intended to please Emma boomeranged, as it so often did.

In 1934, when Emma returned home from her three-month tour of the United States, suffering mightily from both her failed affair with Frank Heiner (the blind osteopath) and her watered-down tour results, Sasha and Emmy thought to cheer her up by giving Bon Esprit a brilliant makeover. Emmy, especially, threw herself into the work of restoring the long-neglected cottage (needless to say, Emma was no housekeeper). Of this homecoming Candace Falk writes: "Emma returned to find Bon Esprit sparkling, flowers in bloom all around, but her senses seemed numbed by the confusion and emptiness [she was now feeling]. . . . Although her letters to Emmy from afar had signaled a new warmth, when she was face to face with this young woman who claimed the affection of her soulmate, she could not contain her jealousy and resentment. No matter how cheerful Emmy and Sasha tried to make Emma's return, Emma could not see beyond her own misery, feeling even more alone in their presence. Her only comment on Emmy's work on [the cottage] was critical. Why, she asked, had Emmy spent so much money on paint?"

With real sorrow, Sasha wrote to Emma's niece Stella: "The surprise of the renovated house and the cleared garden, the most warm welcome, etc, failed to raise her spirits, unfortunately. . . . Even Emmy's spontaneous cheerfulness and my 'celebrated' jokes were powerless to lighten the atmosphere. Indeed, I believe that the cheerfulness was resented. . . . It's too bad, of course, but there is no cure for it."

Emma Goldman never had any real insight into the motive force behind her own behavior. She had spent her life, as every self-styled prophet does, converting her every feeling into the language most useful to the Cause and in time could genuinely not do otherwise. Candace Falk nails it: "Never in her life had Emma allowed herself to feel pain and anger fully without transforming them into disappointment in the failure of her grand vision. . . . In describing the breakup of her marriage [for instance], instead of re-experiencing her sadness, anger, and loneliness, she immediately shifted to a discussion of free love and the young revolutionaries of Russia, and her 'disappointment' in the failure of this ideal." In writing the autobiography, the pain she felt at reliving a life that was irrevocably lost to her was nearly unbearable; it was only by resorting to the high-flown rhetoric she regularly employed in her speeches and in her writing—"the deeps of my consciousness"; "the savage howls of a swaying, jostling pack"; "my heart rose to ecstatic heights"—that she could overwhelm that which threatened to overwhelm her. And overwhelm it she did.

*Living My Life* is a memorable repository of richly recounted history that takes its place among the valued social documents of the late nineteenth and early twentieth centuries. It is not, in the view of this biographer, a work of literature. While the gifts of a natural storyteller are in evidence at every turn, the book is an account of an extraordinarily public life presented by a protagonist whose motives are uniformly heroized and whose embarrassments routinely whitewashed; Emma's account of her love life, for example, is absurdly romanticized, with herself appearing always as one ennobled by emotions of a high-minded order while those of the lovers are at best weak and at worst cowardly. This, of course, goes in spades for the friends and enemies of anarchism, all of whom are idealized or demonized. Nonetheless, as a political memoir *Living My Life* is a superior example of the genre, transcribing as it does the day-by-week-by-month-by-year record of a passionate ideologue for whom devotion to the cause of anarchism is as life's blood.

The book came out in 1931 to mixed reviews in the United States. The common criticism, both from those who attacked and those who celebrated, was the intense emotionalism of the prose. Freda Kirchwey of the *Nation* delivered one of the few judicious reviews. She praised the strong emotion with which it was written—"Herein lies her undeniable power. Her emotion is both intense and universal, her expression of it—in words and actions—unrestrained, her courage completely instinctive"—while adding, "She is contemptuous of any intellectualizing that stands in the way of faith and action. Always she feels first and thinks later—and less." But newspapers and magazines such as the *New York Times*, the *Saturday Review of Literature*, and the *New Yorker* considered *Living My Life* one of the best books of the year. One writer advised his readers to read it "as a human document of the most absorbing interest." Another said, "She belongs to a species which is at least temporarily vanishing . . . an original and picturesque personality." *Time* magazine tipped a patronizing hat: "Everybody admires a fighter who has heart. Now that Emma Goldman's fighting Red career is finished, you may even find it possible to add a kind of warmth to your disapproving admiration of her."

Many a revolutionary is pronounced heroic once the period in which he or she seemed threatening passes. By 1931, when the communists had become the evil other, anarchists were considered quaint. Suddenly those who had been considered potential bomb throwers were figures worthy of nostalgic affection. By 1934, when Franklin Roosevelt signed the piece of paper permitting Emma Goldman to enter the United States for a ninety-day visit, the press was displaying more sentimentality than hostility, although a Depression-tinged bitterness was also in evidence. The range of responses in the papers was actually more revealing of the emotional state of the world than of anything to do with Emma Goldman herself, but certainly it was occasioned by her appearance in the country. The morning after the announcement of her visa, her return was news.

The *Portland Oregonian:* "The times when we thought Emma spelled trouble were truly the halcyon days. We knew not the meaning of trouble."

The Mobile, Alabama, *Press Register:* "The opponent of government in any form, [Emma] has seen government in every country assuming a consistently stronger hold on the individual."

The *Saginaw News:* "Poor Emma [is] . . . likely to be somewhat lonesome when she starts getting about in this country again. There are so very few capitalists left to denounce."

The *Baltimore Sun:* "The nation of anarchists which she knew of old [is] changed to a nation clamoring for regimentation."

Other editors reminisced about the years when "Americans intimidated their children by threatening to turn them over to Emma Goldman unless they were good" and seemed to long for the woman they once considered a public menace.

But Emma would have none of the nostalgia. To the sympathetic audiences she faced that year in the United States—many of whom wished to idolize her as a martyred heroine of a romantically lost cause—she said flatly, "I do not consider myself a suffering martyr. I have followed my bent, lived my life as I chose and no one owes me anything. I'm not more respectable than I ever was. It's you who have become a little more liberal [that is, less radical]." And then she assured them that they could, if only they would, progress *back* to radicalism.

An insightful reporter at the Chicago *Daily News* who heard her speak wrote, "Emma's unabated political intensity led some to view her as a 'she Peter Pan.' She has never grown up emotionally, which means she has not lost the naïve courage and consistency of childhood and adolescence. . . . Fanatics who, like Emma, have rocked the world, are people whose intellects get out in front of their emotional adjustments and stay there." He was wrong in only one regard: it wasn't intellect, it was a depth of spirit—unaltered, unyielding, uncompromised—that was, as it had always been, way out in front.

Returned from America, Emma wandered around Europe, lecturing here and there, but with increasingly unsatisfactory results, both politically and financially. The loss of energy that comes with demoralization began to overtake her. "I am tired to death," she wrote Sasha, "of all the people I have already seen who claimed interest. . . . I see no indication of any real support. . . . Our own people are, as everywhere, ineffectual . . . we have no one of any ability whatever. The groups consist of living corpses. . . . And yet we must go on in our work. We are voices in the wilderness, much more so than forty years ago." The placement of those last two sentences says it all. In the old days they would surely have been reversed.

Yet on she went. In 1935 she returned to London, thinking she could do something useful there, and again plunged into a welter of self-propelled activity, drumming up lectures, meetings, and public events even while she felt herself at loose ends in a world she less and less recognized as her own. Sasha, however, marveled at her powers of recuperation: "The things you manage to do, the numbers of people to see, parties to attend, and at the same time read and prepare lectures—and not to forget, to write long letters! It's astounding." No, no, she wrote back; "More and more I am coming to believe it matters little what any one of us does or leaves undone." His answer: "One must not carry Weltschmerz into his daily life, for in that manner, existence becomes impossible." And then, as though to give her something solid to live by, he wrote her, "Our friendship and comradeship of a lifetime has been to me the most beautiful and inspiring factor in my whole life. And after all, it is given to but few mortals to live as you and I have lived. Notwithstanding all our hardships and sorrows, all persecution and imprisonment—perhaps because of it all—we have lived the lives of our choice. What more can one expect of Life."

On June 27, 1936 (Emma's sixty-seventh birthday), Sasha Berkman, suffering from terminal cancer, committed suicide. His death plunged Emma into true despair, rather than mere depression. Those closest to her feared for her survival; and two, knowing that Emma's will to live could be revived only through involvement in political action, decided to act on her behalf. The Spanish Civil War, which that summer of 1936 was holding the attention of the world, was just the thing to bring her back to herself.

Five years earlier, the Spanish monarchy had been toppled by a popular vote for a republic. The new elected government had brought the country's socialists to power, but their hold on the various volatile elements of Spanish society had proved fragile. By 1933 it was being seriously challenged by Catholics, liberal moderates, and right-wing nationalists. Reluctantly, the various left-wing elements—anarchists, unionists, liberals, and communists—joined hands to form the Popular Front, which carried the national elections in February 1936 by the narrowest of margins. In July, General Francisco Franco led a rebellion of anti–left wing forces within the army, with the aim of establishing a fascist government. The country was at once divided between nationalists and republicans, and civil war broke out. In the immediate aftermath, it was the anarchists among the republicans who dominated the action, seizing factories, communalizing farms, and making self-government an unheard-of reality, particularly in Barcelona. Then, expecting the democratic world to come to its aid, the Popular Front watched in horror as Franco was supplied by Hitler and Mussolini while the republican cause was abandoned. It was precisely this abandonment that stirred individual liberals and radicals across the Western world to take up the cause of the republicans; and within the year the famous International Brigades arrived in Spain to fight on their side.

It was into this state of affairs that Emma's friends sought to insert her. They wrote secretly to Augustine Souchy, founder of the German Anarchist International, urging him to formally solicit her engagement in the war without letting her know that the idea did not originate with him. He did as he was requested, and Emma responded with quickly marshaled fervor, arriving in Barcelona in September. Spain was to provide her with the last cause for anarchist joy that she would know—and the only time in her life that she was to see, on the ground, a little world being run (successfully!) through the application of anarchist principles.

In the midst of civil war, with the anarchists in control in Catalonia, Aragon, and Andalusia, a genuine workers' revolution—composed of republicans, socialists, communists, and Catalan separatists, as well as members of the petite bourgeoisie—came into being and operated successfully for three years: long enough for many European visitors to witness and report on the amazing experiment. Land and industry had been seized and nationalized, and libertarian communes formed in the cities and the country; unlike the "collectives" of Soviet Russia, these were the real thing. The economy was almost entirely under workers' control: farms, factories, shops, public works, hotels and restaurants, businesses of every sort; all had been collectivized and were being managed by the workers, without bosses of any kind. Suddenly, Kropotkin's romantic belief in mutual aid had become a reality. A genuine grassroots democracy had been instituted, with most individuals participating directly in the reorganization of their social and political life. In many places money had been abolished. Payment for labor and services was rendered according to the anarchist-communist principle of "from each according to his ability and to each according to his needs." Coupons were distributed that could be traded in for food, clothing, fuel, whatever else was needed.

Between eight and ten million people took part in this experience, and while it had many detractors with many legitimate objections, most observers responded like George Orwell, who, in *Homage to Catalonia*, wrote: "There was much in this that I did not understand, in some ways I did not even like it, but I recognized it immediately as a state of affairs worth fighting for. . . . [S]o far as one could judge the people were contented and hopeful. There was no unemployment and the price of living was still extremely low. . . . Above all, there was a belief in the revolution and the future, a feeling of having suddenly emerged into an era of equality and freedom. Human beings were trying to behave as human beings and not as cogs in the capitalist machine."

Ernest Hemingway as well (not to mention scores of previously apolitical journalists) wrote eloquently of the amazement and sympathy with which he witnessed—especially in Catalonia—for the first and only time what looked like an egalitarian democracy at work. In industry, on farms, even in military units, the genuineness of social equality moved even inexpressive men to tears.

Emma was welcomed as a friend of the revolution everywhere she went, and once again found herself exhorting large crowds: this time not to rebel but to hold fast. She wrote home to her niece, "I am walking on air. I feel so inspired and so aroused that I am fortunate enough to be here and to be able to render service to our brave and beautiful comrades. . . . [I am] fairly drunk with the sights, the impressions and the spirit of our comrades. . . . One completely forgets oneself and everything of a personal character amidst the life of [this] collective spirit," which, she maintained, was ingrained in the "very texture of the Spanish masses." She wanted to stay in this country forever. So did many others. Women and men far removed from Emma's extravagant style were adopting the same romantic language with which to describe what they were seeing and feeling. For the first time in many years Emma felt herself at one with the world immediately around her. The Spanish anarchists were proving that anarchism was a social philosophy "worth living, fighting and if need be, dying for." No formal defeat, if defeat should come, could ever deprive her of this newly revitalized conviction. "I would rather go down with the revolution if it should come to that than return to Europe, England, or Canada," she wrote a friend. She wished passionately that she could actually be fighting on the front lines: "I never felt my age as I do now."

In January 1937 she returned to London to organize support for the cause of republican Spain, writing to friends all over the world, "I should not have believed such a thing possible had I not seen with my own eyes [their] epic greatness, their defense of Madrid, their superhuman struggle now to defend Catalonia . . . Whatever the outcome of the unequal struggle, the contribution they have already made to the greatness of the [undaunted] human spirit . . . can never die and never be lost." Newspaper articles all over Europe and America echoed these sentiments. The cause of republican Spain had become the common property of all who thrilled to the sight of organized bravery.

The brutality of the war, however, was soul destroying. For the first time in modern warfare the inconceivable was happening: civilian populations—in Madrid, Barcelona, Guernica—were being bombed. This shocking development, combined with the internecine struggle going on within left-wing republican forces, served to strengthen the fascist cause. In May 1937, the factionalism within the Popular Front erupted, and its culmination was a horrifying exchange of gunfire between anarchists and communists that left four hundred dead on the streets of Barcelona and the Soviet-backed communists in control. As the anarchist movement collapsed, and the Soviet Union started taking over, the social revolution was knocked to pieces. Moscow had declared the defeat of Franco primary— forget about worker control—and many anarchists felt they had no choice but to cooperate. It seemed like the Bolshevik takeover all over again.

Emma was beside herself. Only one among many who ar-

gued that the revolution and the war were one and the same—
lose that, she raged, and who cared whether or not the fascists
won?—nonetheless it was her objection to cooperation with the
communists that knew no bounds, and soon her public condemnation of what she called appeasement began to embar-
rass her anarchist comrades. One of these was Mariano Vazquez, secretary of the Spanish anarchist union, the National
Confederation of Labor (CNT), who in an angry letter-writing
exchange with Emma insisted that the anarchists had had no
choice but to cooperate with the communists, who for them
seemed a lesser evil than Franco; besides, he added bitterly, no
revolution in a country like Spain could ever succeed without
that which had steadily been denied them: worldwide prole-
tarian solidarity. Emma, however, would have none of it: they
should have gone on fighting till not one anarchist was left
standing. It was all ashes in her mouth.

"Spain has paralyzed my will and killed my hopes," Emma
now wrote. "It's as though you had wanted a child all your life
and at last, when you had almost given up hope, it had been
given to you—only to die soon after it was born. . . . I have
lived long enough, the agony over the Russian Revolution
was enough for one life. Now the Spanish Revolution is to be
crushed. Life holds nothing else. I feel like one drowning, grab-
bing the air."

But Emma was constitutionally incapable of falling apart.
Feeling helpless, she nonetheless, "in loyalty to the cause,"
organized a Committee to Aid Homeless Spanish Women
and Children in London. It then occurred to her (reasonably
enough) to travel to Canada, where she thought money could
more easily be raised for this new baby of hers. Some growing
alienation from Europe must also have been at work, however,
because she set about cutting all her ties to the continent. She
sold Bon Esprit, where she now felt only "the agony of the dead
past come to life," then she sold her own and Sasha's papers to

the International Institute for Social History in Amsterdam. It was suddenly as though she were accumulating *real* money with which to settle elsewhere.

While Emma was a great one for fantasizing any future that lay immediately before her—she still dreamt of returning to the United States, the only country she'd ever loved—the return to continental North America proved harder to bear than it had ever been before. She had imagined that if she were ensconced in Toronto, among old American connections who would rally to the cause of the Spanish republic, a new life would materialize, one that would not only put her back where she belonged— organizing protest—but enable her to gain a modest amount of financial security. In spite of herself, she still resented the fact that after all the work she had done for the movement she was saddled with the anxiety of having to make a living and could not rely on the comrades to provide for her. In fact, between her deportation and her death twenty long years later, she lived perpetually on the edge of poverty.

At first it seemed as though things were going to work out as she had hoped they would. A Seventieth Birthday Fund was organized for her, and people and birthday wishes came in from all over the world. Among the most precious to her was a cable from Mariano Vazquez, who wrote: "You have understood us and our aim as few who came to our shores have understood us. For this among many other reasons, you have become part of us, never to be forgotten."

Some money was raised, but not nearly enough; and more important, she could not make her cause the cause of those around her. For old American comrades, Hitler and the Jews now loomed infinitely larger than refugees from the Spanish Civil War. This last took her by surprise. All her political life she had insisted that the problem of Jewishness was its retrograde nationalism; antisemitism, she always said, would disappear if only the Jews, individually and as a culture, worked for the achievement of international anarchism. In the face of full-blown Nazism (it was now 1939), she still thought Francisco Franco the only real enemy.

In no time at all the party was over, and she was alone. Not only did all her comrades disappear back into the lives they were living across the border; the Canadian government sought to muffle her voice. She was permitted to speak but not on domestic politics. She could lecture but not on the probability of the coming war. She could write but couldn't find a publisher willing to give her an advance. She continued to work for the Spanish refugees and to have visits with friends and family who traveled to see her, but "I am so terribly cut off from intellectual contact. I grow so depressed and unhappy at times it seems I could not stand it another day." Waves of longing for Sasha threatened daily to drown her.

And then along came the cause of "the Italian chap," as Emma referred to him in her letters, which allowed her to die in harness.

Arthur Bortolotti was an Italian anarchist who had lived in Canada for twenty years but, like most principled anarchists, had failed to take out citizenship papers. Now, in 1939, after a new War Measures Act was passed, he and three other anarchists were arrested for distributing subversive literature and threatened with deportation back to Mussolini's Italy, where they were sure to meet with imprisonment, if not death. The arrest—seen at once as a test for how much censorship was to be enforced in Canada during the coming war—instantly achieved notoriety, and liberals and radicals everywhere registered a protest.

Emma, who had met Bortolotti years before, was drawn to help with the defense of the four anarchists. She was old, and so tired, but immediately began to organize a support committee to exert pressure for their release and raise money to pay for their legal defense. In no time, she found herself "at my old job—trying to help someone out of the clutches of the police." Lecturing and attending meetings for the case, she felt revitalized, and was further heartened to find that the Toronto papers were once again labeling her "the most dangerous woman in the world."

She and Arthur drew close, seeing each other daily, planning, plotting, commiserating. And then, as in the old days, an assortment of comrades working on the case began to gather daily in her apartment. She threw herself into the organizing of this defense as though it were the most significant battle of her life. Until the day he died, Bortolotti spoke of her nobility on his behalf.

On February 13, 1940, the Canadian immigration board ordered the anarchists deported, and an appeal was immediately entered. Four days later, on a snowy evening, in anticipation of a meeting, Emma waited with three comrades in her flat for Arthur, who'd gone to pick up three others. To pass the time they played cards. One of the players took his turn, and Emma cried, "God damn it, why did you lead with that?" These were her last words. She slumped in her chair. She had suffered a massive stroke that left her speechless and paralyzed on one side. When Arthur arrived, he found her lying on her bed, looking terrified, and struggling to get up.

Emma lived three awful months after her stroke—long enough, on the one hand, for the bitter irony of her speechlessness to escape no one, least of all her, but, on the other, to see Arthur Bortolotti's deportation sentence reversed. On May 14, surrounded by Arthur and his friends, she died.

She had always wanted to be buried beside the Haymarket Martyrs in Chicago's Waldheim Cemetery, and, remarkably, the U.S government did not object. Her body was shipped to the States, placed in a hall in downtown Chicago, her coffin draped with the banner of the Spanish anarchists, and covered with flowers that had arrived from all over the world. Thousands of people trooped past the coffin, and at the cemetery chimes from the chapel rang out a requiem.

# Part IV

---

*Legacy*

ON HER SEVENTIETH BIRTHDAY, an admirer told Emma Goldman, "It was not what you did or said that helped me, but what you were, the mere fact of the existence of your spirit which never gives in and fights on no matter how thick is the darkness in the world and in our own little worlds."

No one ever said it better: the spirit that fights on no matter how thick the darkness.

Emma Goldman was not a thinker, she was an incarnation. It was not her gift for theory or analysis or even strategy that made her memorable; it was the extraordinary force of life in her that burned, without rest or respite, on behalf of human integrity. Hers was the sensibility not of the intellectual but of the artist; and she performed like an artist, dramatizing for others what they could hardly articulate for themselves. To hear Emma describe, in language as magnetic as it was illuminating, what the boot felt like on the neck was to feel the mythic quality of organized oppression. It made you *see* yourself in history. That insight eased the heart, cleared the air, clarified the spirit. To clarify was to gain courage; and courage, if nothing else, was an exhilaration. Through Emma's performance, anarchism did what Tolstoy said a work of art should do: it made people love life more.

Anarchism is the political philosophy that comes closest to addressing the anguish of the stifled spirit, and in Emma Goldman it found its visceral embodiment. Social injustice may or may not have been the cause of, or the explanation for, her exorbitant sense of insult in the face of power ill-used, but it surely was its intimate. It was not even the injustice itself that she found so oppressive, it was being forced to *submit* to it without recourse to opposition; that was the human right that was at stake. To accept the denial of that right—the very right that Prometheus, chained to a rock continuously being eaten alive, refused to relinquish—was to surrender something vital to one's humanity: that which supplied the difference between those who walked the earth upright and those who crawled on all fours. What Emma prized above all else was the honor and the glory of the Promethean refusal—and it was with those who shared this value that, all her years, she felt most alive. The world of the utopian anarchist future held much less reality for her than the one in which she fought daily to secure the rights of the rebel and the dissenter.

For this reason alone she loved the United States more than any other country she lived in. On the barricades for international anarchism, Emma nonetheless never stopped being amazed at and delighted by Americans' appetite for protest as, time and again, she saw one part of the body politic or another rise up to claim what the democracy had promised but failed to deliver. With all its capitalist brutality, America was where the rebel seemed most unconquerable. She loved passionately the sight of anarchism being made to serve homegrown U.S. radicalism. She loved it, and she learned from it.

In Emma Goldman we have a prototype of the European anarchist crucially influenced by the American insistence on individuation. Had she been alive in the 1960s she would have been as excited by the rise of the new left and the liberationist movements as they were by her. No sooner had she been rediscovered than it turned out she had written an article, mounted a protest, sat in jail on behalf of nearly every issue on their agendas. For a generation of radicals that dreamed, a hundred years after her birth, of a future in which direct democracy would be practiced and institutional politics abolished, she had become an emblematic figure.

Forty years on she is more than emblematic, she is iconic. Probably the most influential chant of the 1960s and 1970s— the one that most recalls the eloquent demands of the Lyrical Left—is "The personal is political." This is the phrase that for decades has conjured the noble enterprise of struggling against permanent odds to achieve a world in which a healthy respect for the inner life occupies center stage. It is also the phrase that most deserves to be associated—in fear, hope, and excitement—with the legacy of Emma Goldman.

# SELECTED BIBLIOGRAPHY

Avrich, Paul. *Anarchist Portraits*. Princeton: Princeton University Press, 1988.

Chalberg, John C. *Emma Goldman. American Individualist*. 2d ed. New York: Pearson Longman, 2008.

Diggins, John P. *The Rise and Fall of the American Left*. New York: Norton, 1992.

Falk, Candace. *Love, Anarchy, and Emma Goldman*. New York: Holt, Rinehart, and Winston, 1984.

Falk, Candace, ed. *Emma Goldman: A Documentary History*. 2 vols. Berkeley: University of California Press, 2005.

Frankel, Oz. "Whatever Happened to 'Red Emma'? Emma Goldman, from Alien Rebel to American Icon." *Journal of American History* 83, no. 3 (December 1996): 903–42.

Glassgold, Peter, ed. *Anarchy! An Anthology of Emma Goldman's "Mother Earth."* Berkeley, Calif.: Counterpoint, 2001.

Goldman, Emma. *Anarchism and Other Essays*. New York: Mother Earth Publishing, 1910.

————. *My Disillusionment in Russia.* New York: Doubleday, 1923.

————. *Living My Life.* New York: Knopf, 1931.

————. *The Social Significance of the Modern Drama.* Boston: Gorham, 1914.

————. *Voltairine de Cleyre.* Berkeley Heights, N. J.: Oriole, 1932.

Gordon, Linda. *The Moral Property of Women: A History of Birth Control Politics in America.* 3rd ed. Urbana: University of Illinois Press, 2002.

Michels, Tony. *A Fire in Their Hearts.* Cambridge: Harvard University Press, 2005.

Morton, Marian J. *Emma Goldman and the American Left.* New York: Twayne, 1992.

Schorske, Carl E. *Fin-de-Siècle Vienna.* New York: Vintage, 1981.

Shulman, Alix Kates. *To the Barricades.* New York: Crowell, 1971.

Shulman, Alix Kates, ed. *Red Emma Speaks: Selected Writings and Speeches.* New York: Schocken, 1983.

Stansell, Christine. *American Moderns: Bohemian New York and the Creation of a New Century.* New York: Holt, 2002.

Wexler, Alice. *Emma Goldman: An Intimate Life.* New York: Pantheon, 1984.

————. *Emma Goldman in Exile.* Boston: Beacon, 1989.

# INDEX

JEWISH LIVES is a major series of interpretive
biography designed to illuminate the imprint of eminent Jewish
figures upon literature, religion, philosophy, politics, cultural and
economic life, and the arts and sciences. Subjects are paired with
authors to elicit lively, deeply informed books that explore the
breadth and complexity of Jewish experience
from antiquity through the present.

Jewish Lives is a partnership of Yale University Press
and the Leon D. Black Foundation.

Anita Shapira and Steven J. Zipperstein
are series editors.